HAMLYN ALL COLOUR
ITALIAN COOKBOOK

HAMLYN

First published 1993 by Hamlyn.

This edition published in 1997 by Chancellor Press an imprint of
Reed International Books Ltd., Michelin House, 81 Fulham Road, London SW3 6RB
and Auckland, Melbourne, Singapore and Toronto.

Additional recipes by Patrcia Bourne.
Line drawings by Sandra Pond and Will Giles.
Photographs for recipes 1, 12, 21, 24, 25, 28, 29, 31, 33, 39, 41, 43, 45, 50, 53, 57, 61, 66,
71, 80, 81, 82, 89, 90, 101, 103, 108, 109, 133, 135, 137, 139, 143, 147, 149, 151, 154, 156, 157, 175,
187, 189, 190, 191, 193, 195, 204, 207, 215 and 216 by James Murphy; all other photographs
from Reed Consumer Books Picture Library.

ISBN 1 85152 915 2

A CIP catalogue record for this book is available from the British Library

Produced by Mandarin Offset
Printed and bound in China

OTHER TITLES IN THIS SERIES INCLUDE:

Hamlyn All Colour Chinese Cookbook
Hamlyn All Colour Barbecues and Summer Food
Hamlyn All Colour Meals in Minutes
Hamlyn New All Colour Vegetarian Cookbook
Hamlyn All Colour Indian Cookbook
Hamlyn All Colour Teatime Favourites

CONTENTS

USEFUL FACTS AND FIGURES

NOTES ON METRICATION

In this book quantities are given in metric and Imperial measures. Exact conversion from Imperial to metric measures does not usually give very convenient working quantities and so the metric measures have been rounded off into units of 25 grams. The table below shows the recommended equivalents.

Ounces	Approx g to nearest whole figure	Recommended conversion to nearest unit of 25	Ounces	Approx g to nearest whole figure	Recommended conversion to nearest unit of 25
1	28	25	9	255	250
2	57	50	10	283	275
3	85	75	11	312	300
4	113	100	12	340	350
5	142	150	13	368	375
6	170	175	14	396	400
7	198	200	15	425	425
8	227	225	16(1lb)	454	450

Note

When converting quantities over 16 oz first add the appropriate figures in the centre column, then adjust to the nearest unit of 25. As a general guide, 1kg (1000 g) equals 2.2 lb or about 2 lb 3 oz. This method of conversion gives good results in nearly all cases, although in certain pastry and cake recipes a more accurate conversion is necessary to produce a balanced recipe.

Liquid measures

The millilitre has been used in this book and the following table gives a few examples.

Imperial	Approx ml to nearest whole figure	Recommended ml	Imperial	Approx ml to nearest whole figure	Recommended ml
1/4	142	150 ml	1 pint	567	600 ml
1/2	283	300 ml	1 1/2 pints	851	900 ml
3/4	425	450 ml	1 3/4 pints	992	1000 ml (1 litre)

Spoon measures

All spoon measures given in this book are level unless otherwise stated.

Can sizes

At present, cans are marked with the exact (usually to the nearest whole number) metric equivalent of the Imperial weight of the contents, so we have followed this practice when giving can sizes.

Oven temperatures

The table below gives recommended equivalents.

	°C	°F	Gas Mark		°C	°F	Gas Mark
Very cool	110	225	1/4	Moderately hot	190	375	5
	120	250	1/2		200	400	6
Cool	140	275	1	Hot	220	425	7
	150	300	2		230	450	8
Moderate	160	325	3	Very hot	240	475	9
	180	350	4				

NOTES FOR AMERICAN AND AUSTRALIAN USERS

In America the 8-fl oz measuring cup is used. In Australia metric measures are now used in conjunction with the standard 250-ml measuring cup. The Imperial pint, used in Britain and Australia, is 20 fl oz, while the American pint is 16 fl oz. It is important to remember that the Australian tablespoon differs from both the British and American tablespoons; the table below gives a comparison. The British standard tablespoon, which has been used throughout this book, holds 17.7 ml, the American 14.2 ml, and the Australian 20 ml. A teaspoon holds approximately 5 ml in all three countries.

British	American	Australian
1 teaspoon	1 teaspoon	1 teaspoon
1 tablespoon	1 tablespoon	1 tablespoon
2 tablespoons	3 tablespoons	2 tablespoons
3 1/2 tablespoons	4 tablespoons	3 tablespoons
4 tablespoons	5 tablespoons	3 1/2 tablespoons

AN IMPERIAL/AMERICAN GUIDE TO SOLID AND LIQUID MEASURES

Imperial	American	Imperial	American
Solid measures		Liquid measures	
1 lb butter or		1/4 pint liquid	2/3 cup liquid
margarine	2 cups	1/2 pint	1 1/4 cups
1lb flour	4 cups	1/4 pint	2 cups
1 lb granulated or		1 pint	2 1/2 cups
caster sugar	2 cups	1 1/2 pints	3 3/4 cups
1lb icing sugar	3 cups	2 pints	5 cups
8 oz rice	1 cup		(2 1/2 pints)

NOTE: WHEN MAKING ANY OF THE RECIPES IN THIS BOOK, ONLY FOLLOW ONE SET OF MEASURES AS THEY ARE NOT INTERCHANGEABLE.

INTRODUCTION

Italy has a long tradition of influencing and inspiring Western cooking. Even so, the best cooking in Italy is still done, not in famous restaurants or the kitchens of the great and influential, but in the home. The pizza, often eaten by Italians as they stroll along the street, may be one of the most popular foods in Italy, as it is throughout the Western world, but Italian families still gather together at home for the main meal of the day. It is a meal based on excellent quality ingredients bought in local shops and markets. This is the kind of cooking that is the basis of the 240 delicious, easily prepared recipes in the HAMLYN ALL COLOUR ITALIAN COOKBOOK.

Keeping in mind the traditional Italian meal, with its infinitely flexible mixing of courses, the recipes are grouped loosely into food types, making it easy to choose a menu to suit any occasion. An everyday Italian meal generally starts with a *minestra* – soup, pasta or a rice-based dish – followed by a main course of fish, poultry or meat. Vegetables are served with the main course and a cold salad or vegetable dish may follow. The usual end to the meal is cheese or fruit followed by a strong espresso coffee. If the occasion is special in some way, a simple *antipasto* may start the proceedings and a richly impressive dessert climax it.

The recipes here allow for all this wonderfully varied mixing and matching of courses and dishes. Planning a menu is helped by the good colour photograph which accompanies each recipe (including the first recipe in each chapter, the photograph for which is on the book's cover). The servings number with each recipe is an indication of the average number each recipe should serve. The calorie counts are also helpful in planning well-balanced, healthy meals. Remember that pasta, despite adding up to often quite high calorie counts, is a wonderfully nutritious food, needing just an accompanying low-calorie salad to make a complete meal.

As for the basic ingredients in the recipes, they are as authentically Italian as possible. Most of them, including cheeses, sausages and cured meats, fruits and vegetables, oils and vinegars, herbs, spices and flavourings, are sold widely in our supermarkets, either fresh, vacuum-packed, chilled or canned. Many less familiar ingredients are described in the Cook's Tips at the end of recipes.

Various non-perishable ingredients turn up frequently in Italian dishes and are useful storecupboard items. With a selection of the following in the kitchen cupboard, a great range of authentic Italian cooking becomes available at remarkably short notice: pasta – of course, though you will find recipes to make your own in the pasta chapter; rice, especially Italian arborio rice; dried haricot beans and lentils and various canned beans; olive and vegetable oils; wine vinegar; anchovy fillets in oil; olives; capers; tinned Italian 'plum' tomatoes, available whole or chopped; tomato purée, in jars or tubes; dried herbs (in small quantities and replaced often), especially bay leaves, oregano, rosemary and sage. Other essential herbs, basil and parsley, are best fresh.

With such ingredients in the cupboard and the HAMLYN ALL COLOUR ITALIAN COOKBOOK to hand, the rich and flavourful world of Italian cooking is within easy reach.

SOUPS & STARTERS

Salami, cold meats and hams are very much a feature of *antipasti*, the varied collection of hot and cold dishes often served as a first course in Italy. Particularly in the coastal areas, fish is also served in many different ways. Most Italian soups are quite substantial with the addition of a generous sprinkling of grated Parmesan cheese.

1 ONION AND CHEESE SOUP

Preparation time:
30 minutes

Cooking time:
35-40 minutes

Serves 4-6

Calories:
373-249 per portion

YOU WILL NEED:
2-3 tablespoons olive oil, plus extra for frying
1 kg/2 lb onions, sliced
50 g/2 oz plain flour
1.25 litres/2 ¼ pints chicken stock
salt and white pepper
2 slices stale crustless bread cut into 1 cm/½ inch cubes
50 g/2 oz Parmesan cheese, grated
50 g/2 oz Gruyère cheese, cut into small dice

Heat 2-3 tablespoons of oil in a heavy-based pan and add the onions. Reduce the heat and cook the onions until they are soft but without colour. Stir in the flour, mix well and then add the stock a little at a time, stirring well so that a smooth mixture is obtained. Season to taste with salt and white pepper. Bring to the boil and simmer gently for 20 minutes.

Meanwhile, heat some oil in a frying pan. When it is hot, add the bread and fry until golden brown, turning the dice frequently with a spatula so that they colour evenly. Remove from the pan and drain on absorbent kitchen paper.

Purée the soup in a liquidizer or food processor and return to the pan. Just before serving add the Parmesan and Gruyère cheeses. Heat through and cook for about 2-3 minutes, stirring all the time. Check the seasoning and serve immediately in individual bowls with a few croûtons on the top of each one.

2 BEAN AND CABBAGE SOUP

Preparation time:
15 minutes

Cooking time:
about 2¼ hours

Serves 4

Calories:
628 per portion

YOU WILL NEED:
400 g/14 oz dried haricot beans, soaked in lukewarm water overnight
100 g/4 oz streaky bacon, chopped
2 small heads of cabbage, quartered
2 tablespoons cumin seeds
1 bay leaf
salt
4 tablespoons olive oil
2 garlic cloves, sliced
2 tablespoons plain flour
100 g/4 oz cornmeal

Put the drained beans and the bacon in a pan and pour over water to cover. Bring to the boil, cover and cook for 1½ hours, adding more water as necessary. Meanwhile put the cabbage in another pan with the cumin seeds, bay leaf, a little salt and a very little water. Cook for 2-3 minutes, shaking the pan constantly.

Heat half the oil in another pan, add the garlic and fry until brown. Discard the garlic, then stir the flour into the hot oil. Cook for 2 minutes, stirring constantly, then add the cabbage and cook for a further 5 minutes. Transfer the cabbage to the pan containing the beans, add the remaining oil, then the cornmeal a little at a time, stirring well after each addition. Cook gently for 30 minutes, stirring frequently and adding more water or stock if too dry. Add salt if necessary.

■ COOK'S TIP

To peel the onions, place them in a large bowl and cover with boiling water. Leave for 3-4 minutes, cool under the cold tap and the skins will peel off very easily.

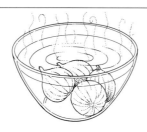

■ COOK'S TIP

This soup was once regarded as a peasant dish but nowadays it is found on the menus of many fashionable restaurants in Trieste.

3 TAGLIATELLE AND BROAD BEAN SOUP

Preparation time:
15 minutes

Cooking time:
about 35 minutes

Serves 4

Calories:
434 per portion

YOU WILL NEED:
300 g/11 oz broad beans, shelled
1.2 litres/2 pints water
salt and pepper
7 tablespoons olive oil
½ onion, chopped
2 garlic cloves, crushed
1 tablespoon chopped parsley
200 g/7 oz tagliatelle, broken up

Put the beans in a large pan with the water, a little salt, the oil, onion, garlic and parsley. Bring to the boil, lower the heat and simmer for 20 minutes or until the beans are tender.

Remove half the beans, mash them and return to the liquid. Add the tagliatelle and salt and pepper to taste, then cook for a further 5-10 minutes until al dente. Serve hot, sprinkled with pepper.

4 ONION SAVOURY

Preparation time:
about 20 minutes,
plus soaking
overnight

Cooking time:
about 35 minutes

Serves 4

Calories:
436 per portion

YOU WILL NEED:
750 g/1 ½ lb onions, sliced
2 tablespoons olive oil
100 g/4 oz bacon, chopped
few basil leaves, chopped
salt and pepper
350 g/12 oz tomatoes, skinned and
   mashed
3 eggs, beaten
75 g/3 oz Parmesan cheese, grated
4 slices hot toasted bread
few basil leaves, to garnish

Put the onions in a bowl, cover with cold water and leave to soak overnight.

Heat the oil in a large heavy pan, add the bacon and fry gently until browned. Drain the onions thoroughly, then add to the pan with the basil and salt and pepper to taste. Cook over low heat for 20 minutes, stirring occasionally.

Add the tomatoes, cover the pan, lower the heat and cook very gently for 10 minutes. Taste and adjust the seasoning. Beat the eggs and Parmesan together, then add to the pan. Remove from the heat immediately and stir vigorously. Put a slice of hot toast in each individual soup bowl, then spoon over the hot savoury. Serve immediately, garnished with basil.

■ COOK'S TIP

Freshly picked broad beans,
straight from the garden, give
the best results. If you have
to buy them in a shop, cook
them as soon as possible
since they do not keep well.

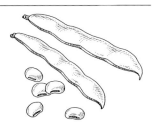

■ COOK'S TIP

Serve this filling soup on a
cold winter weekend after an
energetic week! The best type
of bread to use is one
containing olive oil.

5 ONION SOUP

Preparation time:
15-20 minutes

Cooking time:
1 hour 10 minutes

Serves 6

Calories:
246 per portion

YOU WILL NEED:
2 litres/3 ½ pints chicken stock or water
900 g/2 lb small pickling onions, peeled
   and halved
25 g/1 oz butter
pinch of salt
6 slices hot toasted bread
1 canned red pimento
75 g/3 oz pecorino cheese, grated, to
   serve

Pour the stock or water into a large pan, add the onions, butter and the salt, then bring to the boil. Lower the heat, cover the pan and simmer for 1 hour.

Rub the hot toast with the pimento, then put 1 slice in each of 6 individual soup bowls. Pour the boiling soup over the toast, then sprinkle with the cheese. Serve immediately.

6 SWEETCORN, BARLEY AND BEAN SOUP

Preparation time:
20 minutes, plus
soaking

Cooking time:
about 1 ½ hours

Serves 6

Calories:
358 per portion

YOU WILL NEED:
2 tablespoons olive oil
100 g/4 oz streaky bacon, finely
   chopped
2 garlic cloves, crushed
200 g/7 oz dried borlotti or haricot
   beans, soaked in lukewarm water
   overnight
200 g/7 oz pearl barley, soaked in
   lukewarm water overnight
100 g/4 oz fresh sweetcorn kernels,
   soaked in lukewarm water overnight
2 litres/3 ½ pints light stock
225 g/8 oz potatoes, diced
1 tablespoon chopped parsley
salt and pepper

Heat the oil in a large pan, add the bacon and garlic and fry until golden brown. Drain the beans, barley and sweetcorn and add to the pan with the stock. Bring to the boil, lower the heat and simmer for 45 minutes. Add the potatoes and cook for a further 40 minutes or until the vegetables are tender. Stir in the parsley and salt and pepper to taste. Serve immediately.

■ COOK'S TIP

Pickling onions are picked from the onion plant when it has just formed bulbs and get their name from the fact that they are an ideal size for pickling in jars. Make this *soup in autumn when the onions are available.*

■ COOK'S TIP

If you want to make this soup when fresh sweetcorn is not available, use frozen sweetcorn – this does not of course need soaking.

7 CABBAGE, RICE AND BACON SOUP

Preparation time:
15 minutes

Cooking time:
about 1 hour

Serves 6

Calories:
286 per portion

YOU WILL NEED:
25 g/1 oz butter
½ onion, chopped
50 g/2 oz streaky bacon, chopped
400 g/14 oz cabbage, shredded
1.75 litres/3 pints beef consommé (see Cook's Tip)
salt and pepper
200 g/7 oz rice
1 tablespoon chopped parsley
50 g/2 oz Parmesan cheese, grated

Melt the butter in a large pan, add the onion and bacon and fry gently until lightly coloured. Add the cabbage and fry for 5 minutes, stirring frequently, then stir in the consommé. Bring to the boil and add salt and pepper to taste. Lower the heat, cover the pan and cook gently for 30 minutes.

Stir in the rice and cook for a further 15 minutes, or until tender. Add the parsley, then remove from the heat. Serve hot, with the Parmesan cheese.

8 THICK PULSE SOUP

Preparation time:
20 minutes, plus soaking

Cooking time:
1¾ hours

Serves 6

Calories:
653 per portion

YOU WILL NEED:
100 g/4 oz dried borlotti or red kidney beans
100 g/4 oz dried haricot beans
100 g/4 oz chick peas
100 g/4 oz lentils
7 tablespoons olive oil
100 g/4 oz bacon, chopped
1 carrot, chopped
1 onion, chopped
1 garlic clove, finely chopped
2 litres/3 ½ pints light stock
½ small cabbage, blanched and shredded
225 g/8 oz mushrooms, finely sliced
salt and pepper
225 g/8 oz farfalle
100 g/4 oz pecorino cheese, grated

Soak the pulses in lukewarm water overnight. Drain and put in a large pan. Cover with water and bring to the boil. Cover the pan and simmer for 1¼ hours.

Heat the oil in a large heavy pan. Add the bacon, carrot, onion and garlic, and fry gently for 5 minutes. Add the stock and bring to the boil. Add the cabbage and simmer for 5 minutes. Drain the pulses and add to the pan with the mushrooms and salt and pepper. Stir well, then add the pasta and cook for a further 15 minutes, or until the pasta is tender. Sprinkle with the cheese and serve immediately.

■ COOK'S TIP

Put 1 kg/2 ¼ lb lean beef, 1 onion, ½ celery stick in a large pan. Add 1.75 litres/3 pints water and a little salt. Bring to the boil slowly and skim. Cover and cook just below simmering point for 5-6 hours. Strain through a muslin-lined sieve. Cool, then remove the fat from the top.

■ COOK'S TIP

To blanch the cabbage, immerse it in rapidly boiling water for 2 minutes. Remove from the pan and plunge into ice-cold water.

9   ANCHOVY DIP

Preparation time:
5-10 minutes, plus
preparing vegetables

Cooking time:
15-20 minutes

Serves 6

Calories:
324 per portion
(excluding vegetables)

YOU WILL NEED:
150 ml/ ¼ pint olive oil
3 garlic cloves, crushed
1 × 50 g/2 oz can anchovies, drained
  and roughly chopped
75 g/3 oz unsalted butter
bowl of sliced raw vegetables

Heat the oil in a small frying pan. Add the garlic and anchovies
and simmer over low heat for 15 minutes, stirring occasionally.
Add the butter and stir until melted.

   To serve, stand the frying pan over a fondue burner or spirit
lamp at the table. Guests then dip the vegetables into the hot
sauce.

10   PASTA MINESTRONE

Preparation time:
15 minutes

Cooking time:
50 minutes

Serves 6

Calories:
150 per portion

YOU WILL NEED:
1 tablespoon sunflower oil
1 large onion, chopped
1 garlic clove, chopped
2 carrots, thinly sliced
2 tender celery sticks, thinly sliced
1 large potato, diced
1.5 litres/2 ¾ pints Beef consommé
  (recipe 7)
350 g/12 oz tomatoes, skinned and
  sliced
1 bouquet garni
salt and pepper
100 g/4 oz wholemeal short-cut
  macaroni
175 g/6 oz cooked dried beans
2 courgettes, cut into matchstick strips
3 tablespoons chopped parsley
grated Parmesan cheese, to serve

Heat the oil in a large pan. Fry the onion and garlic over a
moderate heat for 4-5 minutes, stirring once or twice. Add the
carrots, celery and potato, pour on the stock and add the
tomatoes. Add the bouquet garni and season with salt and
pepper. Bring to the boil, cover the pan and simmer for 30
minutes, stirring occasionally.

   Add the macaroni, beans and courgettes, return to the boil,
cover and cook for a further 15 minutes. Taste and adjust the
seasoning. Discard the bouquet garni and stir in the parsley.
Serve hot, with the cheese handed separately.

■ COOK'S TIP

*Suitable raw vegetables
include green peppers,
carrots, turnips, celery and
Jerusalem artichokes. Be sure
to have a good supply of
paper napkins for guests.*

■ COOK'S TIP

*After the soup has simmered
for 30 minutes, allow to
cool. It can be frozen for up
to 3 months. Defrost at
room temperature for 4-5
hours and reheat gently*

*before adding the macaroni,
beans and courgettes and
continuing as in above
recipe.*

11 WHITEBAIT SOUP

Preparation time:
10 minutes

Cooking time:
about 35 minutes

Serves 4

Calories:
288 per portion

YOU WILL NEED:
1 litre/1 ¾ pints fish stock
350 g/12 oz fresh peas, shelled
150 g/5 oz vermicelli or capelli d'angelo
225 g/8 oz whitebait
1 egg, beaten
salt and pepper

Pour the stock into a large pan and bring to the boil. Add the peas and simmer for 20 minutes. Add the vermicelli or capelli d'angelo and whitebait and cook until almost tender. Stir in the egg and salt and pepper to taste; cook for 1 minute. Serve immediately.

12 ROMAN BEAN SOUP

Preparation time:
15 minutes, plus soaking

Cooking time:
2-3 hours

Serves 4-6

Calories:
335-223 per portion

YOU WILL NEED:
1 stick celery, chopped
1 large carrot, chopped
1 large onion, chopped
2 × 400 g/14 oz cans red kidney beans
1 tablespoon olive oil
1 × 400 g/14 oz can chopped tomatoes
2 tablespoons chopped parsley
2 garlic cloves, chopped
½-1 teaspoon chopped rosemary
600-900 ml/1-1 ½ pints chicken stock
   or water
salt and pepper
90 g/3 oz Arborio rice
25-40 g/1-1 ½ oz grated Parmesan
   cheese

Simmer the celery, carrot and onion in 2 canfuls water 15 minutes. Add the drained beans, reserving a cupful.

Meanwhile, heat the oil in a pan and add the tomatoes, parsley and garlic and cook gently until the mixture thickens. Add rosemary and salt and pepper to taste and stir this mixture into the beans and vegetables and cook until tender. Purée in a liquidizer or food processor.

Make the purée up to 1.5 litres/2½ pints with stock or water. Season to taste. Return to the pan and add the rice. Bring to the boil and cook for 10-12 minutes until the rice is cooked. Add the reserved beans, and adjust the consistency of the soup. This is a very thick soup. Heat through and serve hot with the Parmesan handed separately.

■ COOK'S TIP

Make stock from the bones and trimmings of white fish. Freeze in different quantities for future use. Well-reduced fish stock can be frozen in ice-cube trays.

■ COOK'S TIP

To use dried beans: soak 225 g/8 oz red beans overnight, drain, cover with fresh cold water, bring to boil and boil rapidly 15 minutes to prevent toxins forming. Add vegetables (except tomatoes) and simmer 2-2½ hours, without salt. Proceed with recipe, reserving a cupful of beans before puréeing the rest.

13 TOMATO SOUP WITH CROUTONS

Preparation time:
25 minutes

Cooking time:
40 minutes

Serves 4

Calories:
308 per portion

YOU WILL NEED:
4 tablespoons olive oil
1 onion, chopped
3 garlic cloves, crushed
800 g/1 ¾ lb tomatoes, skinned and
    chopped
1 litre/1 ¾ pints chicken stock
salt and pepper
225 g/8 oz stale bread, crusts removed,
    diced
few basil leaves, chopped

Heat half the oil in a large pan, add the onion and garlic and fry gently for 5 minutes. Add the tomatoes and cook for 5 minutes, then gradually stir in the stock. Add salt and pepper to taste, then simmer for 30 minutes.

Meanwhile, heat the remaining oil in a frying pan, add the bread cubes and fry, turning, until crisp and golden.

Add the basil and croûtons to the soup and serve immediately.

14 SORREL SOUP

Preparation time:
15 minutes

Cooking time:
20 minutes

Serves 4

Calories:
251 per portion

YOU WILL NEED:
50 g/2 oz butter
2 onions, chopped
450 g/1 lb potatoes, chopped
salt and pepper
900 ml/1 ½ pints chicken stock
225 g/8 oz sorrel leaves, shredded
4 tablespoons single cream
4 teaspoons snipped chives

Melt the butter in a saucepan, add the onion and potatoes and cook gently, covered, for about 10 minutes, stirring occasionally. Add the chicken broth with salt and pepper, and bring to the boil. Simmer, uncovered, for a further 5 minutes, or until the potatoes are tender. Add the sorrel leaves and cook for a further 5 minutes more. Blend the soup in a liquidizer or food processor until smooth.

Pour the soup into individual bowls and swirl a tablespoon of cream into each. Sprinkle with chives.

■ COOK'S TIP

*If cooking for vegetarians,
use a flavoursome vegetable
stock instead of the chicken
stock to make this soup.*

■ COOK'S TIP

*If fresh sorrel is difficult to
obtain, replace with
watercress. Discard any
discoloured leaves or coarse
stems.*

15 MINESTRONE

Preparation time:
25 minutes

Cooking time:
about 1 hour

Serves 4

Calories:
325 per portion

YOU WILL NEED:
olive oil
1 garlic clove, cut into 3-4 pieces
50 g/2 oz rindless streaky bacon (unsliced), roughly chopped
450 g/1 lb prepared mixed vegetables, such as carrots, celery, leeks, courgettes, cabbage or spinach, roughly chopped
2 ripe tomatoes, roughly chopped
2 potatoes, diced
small bunch of parsley, roughly chopped
salt and pepper
100 g/4 oz canned cannellini beans
100 g/4 oz pasta (ditalini, conchigliette)
50 g/2 oz Parmesan cheese, grated

Coat the bottom of a large saucepan with olive oil and fry the garlic gently until golden and the bacon until crispy. Add the vegetables and parsley with enough water to cover them. Season to taste and simmer gently for about 40 minutes until all the vegetables are cooked and have combined into a thickish soup.

Add the canned beans and enough water to thin down the soup so that it will not become too thick while cooking the pasta. Bring the soup to the boil and add the pasta. Cook according to the type of pasta used. Serve with the grated Parmesan.

16 SOUP WITH PASTA SHAPES

Preparation time:
25 minutes

Cooking time:
8-9 minutes

Serves 4

Calories:
265 per portion

YOU WILL NEED:
200 g/7 oz plain flour
salt
2 eggs, beaten
40 g/1 ½ oz Parmesan cheese, grated
1.5 litres/2 ¾ pints well flavoured beef stock

Sift the flour with ¼ teaspoon salt on to a work surface and make a well in the centre. Add the eggs and Parmesan, then mix together to a smooth dough.

Flatten the dough with a rolling pin and roll out to a 3 mm/⅛ inch thickness. Cut into a 1 cm/½ inch wide strips using a tooth-edged rotary cutter, then cut the strips into pieces 2.5 cm/1 inch long. Pinch each strip in the middle to give a butterfly shape.

Bring the stock to the boil in a large pan, add the butterfly shapes and cook for 6-7 minutes. Serve immediately.

■ COOK'S TIP

Minestrone is best made the previous day though the pasta should be added just before serving. For dieters or those unable to eat fried foods, boil the vegetables with 1-2 pieces of the rind of a hard cheese instead of the bacon and garlic. Add 2 tablespoons of olive oil to the finished soup, before the pasta is added.

■ COOK'S TIP

The freshly made pasta shapes give this soup an authentic taste. Use pinking shears to cut the dough if you do not have a tooth-edged rotary cutter.

17 FISH SOUP

Preparation time:
25 minutes

Cooking time:
30 minutes

Serves 4

Calories:
282 per portion

YOU WILL NEED:
750 g/1 ½ lb scallops or cockles (see Cook's Tip)
200 ml/7 fl oz water
2 canned anchovy fillets, drained
2 garlic cloves
2 tablespoons olive oil
3-4 tablespoons chopped parsley
350 g/12 oz tomatoes, skinned and sliced
salt and pepper
4 slices hot toasted bread

Put the prepared scallops or cockles in a pan with the water. Cover the pan and cook until the shells open, then remove the fish from the shells and set aside. Sieve the cooking liquid and reserve.

Mince the anchovies with the garlic, then put in a large pan with the oil and parsley and cook gently for 5 minutes. Add the tomatoes and salt and pepper to taste, then add the scallops and the reserved cooking liquid making it up to 1 litre/1¾ pints with water. Bring to the boil and cook for 15 minutes.

Place a slice of toast in each soup bowl and pour over the soup. Serve immediately.

18 PASTA AND LENTIL SOUP

Preparation time:
20 minutes, plus soaking

Cooking time:
about 1 hour

Serves 4

Calories:
394 per portion

YOU WILL NEED:
225 g/8 oz small dried lentils
salt
175 g/6 oz canned tomatoes
olive oil
2 garlic cloves, cut into 3-4 pieces
small bunch of parsley, roughly chopped
225 g/8 oz pasta (tubetti, pasta mista)

Put the lentils into a large bowl and add enough water to come a good 5 cm/2 in above the level of the lentils. Leave to soak overnight.

Drain the water off the lentils and put them into a large saucepan, adding enough water to come about 5 cm/2 in above the level of the lentils. Add 1 rounded teaspoon of salt, bring to the boil and simmer until the lentils are three-quarters cooked. The time will vary considerably, depending on the quality and type of lentils used.

Meanwhile, crush the tomatoes or blend them briefly in a liquidizer. Coat the base of a pan with olive oil and gently fry the garlic until golden. Add the tomatoes and half the parsley and simmer gently for about 10 minutes, until the tomato is cooked, adding salt to taste.

When the lentils are ready, pour the sauce into the lentils, add a little water if necessary, enough to cover the pasta, then bring to the boil and add the pasta. Cook according to the type of pasta used. Serve garnished with the remaining parsley.

▮ COOK'S TIP

Scrub the scallops or cockles under cold running water and then drain before putting in a pan. Keep an old nailbrush or toothbrush for cleaning shellfish.

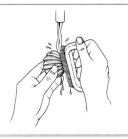

▮ COOK'S TIP

Check the lentils, if bought loose, for grit and foreign bodies. The lentils can be cooked and the sauce made the previous day and the pasta added before serving.

19 SMALL PASTA IN CONSOMME

Preparation time:
30 minutes, plus
standing

Cooking time:
3¼ hours

Serves 6

Calories:
144 per portion

YOU WILL NEED:
2 carrots, trimmed
1 celery stick, halved
1 medium potato, halved
1 ripe tomato, halved
1 onion, halved
small bunch of parsley, rinsed
½ chicken or boiling fowl, rinsed
400 g/14 oz brisket of beef, rinsed
1 teaspoon salt
50 g/2 oz very small pasta per person,
*   such as anellini or capellini*
65 g/2½ oz Parmesan cheese, grated

Make the consommé the day before serving. Put all the ingredients, except for the pasta and parmesan in a large saucepan and add enough water to cover the contents amply and to come three-quarters of the way up the sides of the pan. Bring the water to the boil and simmer very slowly for about 3 hours, topping up with more boiling water if the level falls below that of the meat.

Remove the meat from the pan and strain the consommé through a fine sieve. Leave to stand overnight and when completely cold skim the fat off the surface. Bring the strained consommé to the boil and add the pasta. Cook according to the type of pasta used. Add a little cold water.

Serve with grated Parmesan.

20 CHICK PEA SOUP

Preparation time:
about 25 minutes,
plus soaking

Cooking time:
2¼ hours

Serves 6

Calories:
624 per portion

YOU WILL NEED:
450 g/1 lb chick peas
1 teaspoon bicarbonate of soda
50 g/2 oz raw ham or bacon
½ onion, peeled
1 garlic clove
1 tablespoon chopped parsley
pinch of dried marjoram
50 g/2 oz butter
2 tablespoons olive oil
225 g/8 oz tomatoes, skinned and
*   chopped*
2 litres/3½ pints water
salt and pepper
225 g/8 oz cotechino or other fresh
*   pork sausage, chopped*
1 head of chicory, separated into leaves
6 slices hot toasted bread
75 g/3 oz pecorino cheese, grated

Put the chick peas in a large bowl. Add the soda and cover with cold water. Mix well and leave to soak for 24 hours.

Mince the ham with the onion and garlic, then put in a large pan with the herbs, butter and oil. Cook gently for 6-7 minutes, stirring frequently. Drain the chick peas and add to the pan with the tomatoes and water. Add salt to taste, bring to the boil, then add the sausage. Cover the pan and simmer for 1½ hours. Add the chicory and simmer for a further 30 minutes. Place a slice of toast in each soup bowl. Add the cheese to the soup with pepper, then pour over the toast.

■ COOK'S TIP

The cold water is added to the consommé to cool it down slightly so that the Parmesan, when added does not melt and stick to the bottom of the dish.

■ COOK'S TIP

Thick pulse soups are synonymous with peasant-style cooking, and the regions of Marche and Abruzzi & Molise are noted for their homely minestre — *soups made thick with vegetables and chick peas.*

21 CHICKEN LIVER CROSTINI

Preparation time:
15-20 minutes

Cooking time:
20-30 minutes

Serves 4

Calories:
428 per portion

YOU WILL NEED:
50 g/2 oz butter
1 small onion, finely chopped
1-2 garlic cloves, crushed
225 g/8 oz chicken livers, trimmed of
    all sinew
2 anchovy fillets
1 tablespoon cream
2-3 tablespoons Marsala
salt and pepper
pinch paprika
12 × 1 cm/½ inch slices bread cut
    diagonally from a small French loaf
olive oil for frying
2-3 extra garlic cloves, halved

Heat the butter in a frying pan and cook the onion and garlic until soft but without colour. Add the chicken livers and cook gently for about 10 minutes until they are just coloured through, then add the anchovy fillets. Purée the liver mixture in a food processor or liquidizer until smooth. Add the cream and sufficient Marsala to give a soft spreadable consistency. Season to taste. Keep hot.

Fry the bread slices in hot olive oil until golden brown on both sides. Rub the garlic over one surface of each slice of bread and cover with the liver pâté. Sprinkle a little chopped parsley over each slice just before serving. Serve hot.

22 PARMA HAM WITH MELON

Preparation time:
5 minutes, plus
chilling

Serves 6-8

Calories:
50-37 per portion

YOU WILL NEED:
1 ripe melon
6-8 thin slices Parma ham

Chill the melon for 1 hour in the refrigerator. Cut the melon into 6 or 8 slices and remove the seeds. Place a portion of melon on each of 6 or 8 individual serving plates. Drape a slice of ham over each piece of melon. Serve immediately.

■ COOK'S TIP

Instead of frying the bread, rub the garlic over each slice of bread, then dip the bread into olive oil and place on a baking tray. Bake in a preheated hot oven (230 C, 450 F, gas 8) for 12-15 minutes or until golden brown. Turn once or twice during baking so that the bread colours on both sides.

■ COOK'S TIP

This classic Italian antipasto is based on a superb-quality raw ham which has been cured near Parma for centuries. Try figs as an alternative to melon.

23 BAKED PEPPERS WITH ANCHOVIES

Preparation time:
25 minutes

Cooking time:
35-40 minutes

Oven temperature:
190 C/375 F/gas 5

Serves 4

Calories:
175 per portion

YOU WILL NEED:
2 green peppers
2 red peppers
3 garlic cloves, finely chopped
4 small tomatoes, sliced
8 anchovy fillets
4 tablespoons olive oil
quartered lemon slices, to serve

Place the whole peppers under the grill, turning occasionally until the skin is charred. Cool slightly, then remove the skin with a small sharp knife. Cut each pepper in quarters and remove the seeds.

Put the peppers on a greased baking tray, skinned side down. Sprinkle with the chopped garlic and arrange a slice of tomato over the top of each piece. Halve each anchovy fillet crossways, then lengthways, and arrange two pieces of anchovy over each tomato. Drizzle over the oil.

Bake in a preheated oven for 30 minutes until the peppers are just cooked. Serve hot or cold with lemon slices to garnish.

24 BEAN AND TUNA FISH SALAD

Preparation time:
15-20 minutes

Serves 4

Calories:
287 per portion

YOU WILL NEED:
1 × 450 g/1 lb can cannellini beans or red beans, drained
3 tablespoons olive oil
2 tablespoons lemon juice
salt and pepper
3-4 spring onions, chopped
1 × 200 g/7 oz can tuna fish, drained and broken into chunks
2 tablespoons chopped parsley

Rinse the beans under the cold tap and leave in a colander to drain until dry, then place in a salad bowl.

Mix together the oil and lemon juice, and season to taste with salt and pepper. Stir the chopped spring onions into the beans, pour over the oil and lemon juice and mix well.

Place the tuna fish on top of the beans and sprinkle the chopped parsley over. Cover with clingfilm and refrigerate until required.

■ COOK'S TIP

Choose shiny, firm peppers and reject any with even a slightly wrinkled skin as this is an indication they are past their prime.

■ COOK'S TIP

This salad can be served on individual plates. Arrange some lettuce leaves on each plate, pile some of the beans in the centre and complete the salad as above.

25   MIXED ANTIPASTI

Preparation time:
20 minutes

Serves 4

Calories:
309 per portion

YOU WILL NEED:
100 g/4 oz or 4 slices smoked salmon
1 × 225 g/8 oz can asparagus spears
1 × 200 g/7 oz can tuna, drained
1 × 120 g/4 ½ oz can sardines
2 hard-boiled eggs, shelled and
    quartered
100-175 g/4-6 oz shelled prawns
a little olive oil
salt and pepper

Wrap 3-4 spears of asparagus in each slice of smoked salmon.

Arrange all the ingredients decoratively on a large plate. Season with salt and pepper and dribble a little oil over the fish. Cover with clingfilm and refrigerate until required.

26   FLAMED TAGLIATELLE WITH YOGURT

Preparation time:
10 minutes

Cooking time:
10 minutes

Serves 4

Calories:
606 per portion

YOU WILL NEED:
350 g/12 oz wholemeal tagliatelle
salt and pepper
50 g/2 oz butter
3 tablespoons brandy
150 ml/¼ pint plain yogurt
65 g/2 ½ oz Parmesan cheese, grated
50 g/2 oz walnut halves, to garnish

Cook the tagliatelle in plenty of boiling, salted water for about 10 minutes, or according to the directions on the packet, until it is just tender. Drain, refresh in hot water, and drain again.

Melt the butter in a pan and toss the tagliatelle to coat thoroughly. Pour on the brandy, stir well and light it, to burn off the alcohol.

Stir in the yogurt and cheese, and season with plenty of black pepper. Garnish with the walnuts and serve immediately.

■ COOK'S TIP

The original Italian name for this dish is Antipasto Volente. Volente is roughly translated to mean 'how it comes' so you can use any selection of seafood, sliced
mozzarella cheese, Parma ham and/or salami. Slices of melon, sliced fresh figs and artichoke hearts could also be included.

■ COOK'S TIP

This unusual dish is quickly made and ideal for serving as an appetizer before a cold main course. Other pasta shapes may be cooked in the same way.

27 SPINACH AND RICOTTA TARTLETS

Preparation time:
25 minutes

Cooking time:
30-35 minutes

Oven temperature:
200 C/400 F/gas 6

Makes 4

Calories:
354 per tartlet

YOU WILL NEED:
100 g/4 oz plain flour
pinch of salt
50 g/2 oz butter
2 tablespoons water
FOR THE FILLING
100 g/4 oz frozen chopped spinach,
  thawed
200 g/7 oz ricotta or curd cheese
4 teaspoons grated Parmesan cheese
2-3 pinches nutmeg
2 eggs, beaten
4 tablespoons single cream
salt and pepper

Put the flour and salt in a bowl. Add the butter, cut into small pieces, and rub in until the mixture resembles fine bread-crumbs. Add the water and mix to a firm dough. Turn out on to a floured surface and knead lightly.

Divide the dough in four. Roll out each piece to line a 10 cm/4 inch tartlet case. Place the cases on a baking tray, prick the pastry with a fork and bake in a preheated oven for 10 minutes.

Put all the filling ingredients in a bowl and mix well. Pour into the pastry cases and return to the oven for a further 20-25 minutes until the filling has just set. Serve warm or cold.

28 FRIED LITTLE PIZZA PIES

Preparation time:
30-40 minutes, plus
rising

Cooking time:
4-5 minutes per
batch

Serves 4-6

Calories:
776-517 per portion

YOU WILL NEED:
7 tablespoons olive oil
1 garlic clove, crushed
350 g/12 oz onions, sliced
1 × quantity Basic pizza dough (recipe
  159), risen
50 g/2 oz anchovy fillets, roughly
  chopped
75 g/3 oz black olives, pitted and
  roughly chopped
1-2 tablespoons capers, chopped
black pepper
extra oil for frying
1 × quantity Tomato sauce (recipe 81)

Heat 3-4 tablespoons olive oil in a pan and cook the garlic and onion over a gentle heat until they are soft and lightly coloured.

Place the dough on a lightly floured board and work in 2 tablespoons of olive oil. Roll the dough out thinly and cut out rounds with an 8-9 cm/3-3½ inch pastry cutter. Place a portion of the onion in the centre of each circle with some of the anchovies, black olives and capers. Brush around the edge with water. Fold the dough over and press around the edge with a fork to seal well.

Fry the pizzas in batches in shallow or deep hot fat until they are golden brown on both sides. Sprinkle a little salt over just before serving and serve as hot as possible, with the Tomato sauce served separately.

■ COOK'S TIP

You can double the ingredients given for the pastry and use the surplus to make a flan case which can then be frozen for another occasion.

■ COOK'S TIP

These Pizza pies can also be baked in the oven. Brush them with oil on both sides and place on a baking tray, leaving room for them to rise. Leave in a warm place *for about 30 minutes, then bake in a preheated hot oven (230 C, 450 F, gas 8) for 10-15 minutes, until crisp and golden brown.*

FISH & SHELLFISH

In general, the Italians treat their fish simply, with fewer rich sauces than the French like. Fish is often marinated before being grilled or baked. Not surprisingly, pasta plays an important part in Italian fish cookery. This chapter includes recipes for some of the more unusual fish and shellfish found on fish counters.

29 SARDINES WITH PINE NUTS AND ANCHOVIES

Preparation time:
30-35 minutes

Cooking time:
40-50 minutes

Oven temperature:
180 C/350 F/gas 4

Serves 4

Calories:
749 per portion

YOU WILL NEED:
75-100 ml/2 ½-3 fl oz olive oil
225 g/8 oz fresh white breadcrumbs
40 g/1 ½ oz sultanas, soaked in hot
    water and drained
40 g/1 ½ oz pine nuts
1 tablespoon chopped parsley
1 × 40 g/1 ½ oz can anchovies, drained
    and chopped
pinch nutmeg
salt and pepper
750 g/1 ½ lb sardines with heads and
    backbones removed
approximately 12 bay leaves
4 tablespoons lemon juice

Heat 4-5 tablespoons oil in a frying pan and fry half the breadcrumbs over a moderate heat, turning them frequently with a metal spatula until they are a light golden brown. Remove from the heat and add the sultanas, pine nuts, parsley, anchovies and nutmeg. Season to taste with salt and pepper.

Place a little of the mixture inside each sardine and press the sides together to close. Arrange rows of sardines in a single layer in a large oiled oven-to-table dish. Place half a bay leaf between each sardine. Sprinkle the remainder of the breadcrumbs and the oil over the top and bake in a preheated oven for 30 minute. Sprinkle the lemon juice over the top just before serving. Serve hot.

30 WHITEBAIT FRITTERS

Preparation time:
15 minutes

Cooking time:
about 10 minutes

Serves 4

Calories:
482 per portion

YOU WILL NEED:
200 g/7 oz plain flour
salt and pepper
about 300 ml/ ½ pint lukewarm water
450 g/1 lb whitebait
vegetable oil for deep-frying
4 lemon wedges, to serve

Sift the flour with a pinch of salt and pepper into a bowl. Add enough lukewarm water to obtain a thick coating batter, beating vigorously until smooth. Add the whitebait to the batter and stir until thoroughly coated.

Heat the oil in a deep-fryer. Add the whitebait, a few at a time, and deep-fry until golden brown and crisp. Drain on absorbent kitchen paper and keep hot while frying the remainder. Serve with lemon wedges.

■ COOK'S TIP

If fresh sardines are not available, sprats or small pilchards could be used instead.

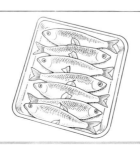

■ COOK'S TIP

To obtain a batter of the right consistency, add only a little of the liquid in the beginning. Then add more liquid and beat until little bubbles appear. Batter can *be made in a blender or food processor, if preferred.*

31 SQUID WITH SPINACH AND TOMATOES

Preparation time:
30-35 minutes

Cooking time:
50-60 minutes

Serves 4

Calories:
266 per portion

YOU WILL NEED:
2-3 tablespoons olive oil
1 medium onion, chopped
1-2 garlic cloves, crushed
1 fresh red chilli, chopped (recipe 53)
1 stick celery, chopped
2 tablespoons chopped parsley
600 g/1 ¼ lb squid, cleaned and cut into
   1 cm/½ inch slices
2 teaspoons plain flour
100 g/4 oz mushrooms, quartered or
   thickly sliced
350 g/12 oz large tomatoes, peeled,
   seeded and chopped
450 g/1 lb fresh spinach, chopped
300 ml/10 fl oz dry white wine
salt and pepper

Heat the oil in a large pan and add the onions, garlic, chilli and celery and cook gently until the onion is golden brown.

Add the parsley and squid and cook gently for a further 10 minutes. Stir in the flour, mix well and then add the mushrooms, tomatoes, spinach and white wine. Season to taste with salt and pepper. Cover and simmer gently for about 30 minutes or until the squid is nearly cooked, then remove the lid and simmer until the sauce thickens and the squid is completely tender. Check the seasoning and pour into a hot serving dish. Serve hot.

▪ COOK'S TIP

Squid may be bought already cleaned; if not your fishmonger may do it for you. Squid must be cooked very gently if it is not to become rubbery. Length of cooking time will depend on size. For the best results with this dish, choose small squid.

32 SEAFOOD CASSEROLE

Preparation time:
20-25 minutes

Cooking time:
about 1 hour

Serves 6

Calories:
332 per portion

YOU WILL NEED:
4 tablespoons olive oil
1 onion, chopped
1 garlic clove, chopped
1 piece of canned pimento, chopped
450 g/1 lb tomatoes, skinned, seeded
   and chopped
4 tablespoons white wine or water
salt and pepper
1.25 kg/2 ½ lb mixed fish, cleaned,
   filleted and cut into pieces if large
   (see Cook's Tip)
6 slices hot toasted bread

Heat half the oil in a large flameproof casserole, add the onion, garlic and pimento and fry gently for 5 minutes. Add the tomatoes, wine or water, and the salt and pepper to taste. Bring slowly to the boil.

If using squid, sauté it in the remaining oil for 4-5 minutes, then add to the tomato mixture. Cover and simmer for 30 minutes. Add the remaining fish, cover and simmer for 15 minutes or until all the fish are tender.

Place a slice of toast in each individual soup bowl and pour over the fish stew. Serve immediately.

▪ COOK'S TIP

For this Sardinian seafood casserole, choose a mixture of fish with different textures, such as squid, sole, halibut, red mullet and eel.

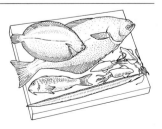

33 MARINATED FRIED SKATE

Preparation time:
20-30 minutes, plus
marinating

Cooking time:
25-30 minutes

Serves 4

Calories:
700 per portion

YOU WILL NEED:

750 g-1 kg/1 ½-2 lb skate wings, cut
   into pieces
salt and pepper
120 ml/4 fl oz white wine vinegar
120 ml/4 fl oz olive oil
1 medium onion, sliced
1 bay leaf
sprig of fresh thyme
3 eggs, beaten
4-6 tablespoons plain flour
oil for deep frying
4-5 sprigs parsley, washed and dried
1-2 lemons, sliced or quartered

Place the skate in a large pan, cover with water, add 1 table-spoon salt. Bring to the boil and simmer gently for 10 minutes. Cool, then remove from the water and drain well. Remove any thick pieces of bone and place the fish in a shallow dish.

Meanwhile, make the marinade. Mix together the vinegar and olive oil with 1 teaspoon salt and ¼ teaspoon pepper. Place the onion, bay leaf and thyme on the fish and pour over the vinegar and oil. Leave for 2-3 hours, turning the fish gently from time to time. Drain and dry the fish well.

Heat the oil to 180-190 C/350-375 F or until a cube of bread browns in 90 seconds. Dip each piece of fish into the beaten eggs and then into the flour and deep fry until golden brown. Drain on absorbent kitchen paper and place on a hot serving dish. Fry the parsley in the hot oil. Arrange on the dish with the fish and garnish with the lemon.

34 SARDINIAN SEAFOOD SALAD

Preparation time:
15 minutes, plus
standing and chilling

Cooking time:
10 minutes

Serves 4

Calories:
483 per portion

YOU WILL NEED:

225 g/8 oz wholemeal macaroni
25 g/1 oz butter
50 g/2 oz mushrooms
100 g/4 oz cooked and shelled mussels
100 g/4 oz peeled, cooked prawns
1 small can anchovies, drained
3 tomatoes, cut into wedges
FOR THE DRESSING
5 tablespoons olive oil
1 tablespoon lemon juice
1 tablespoon wine vinegar
1 garlic clove, crushed
salt and pepper

First, make the dressing: mix together the oil, lemon juice, vinegar, garlic and salt and pepper to taste. Add the oregano. Allow the dressing to stand for 1 hour for the flavours to blend.

Cook the macaroni in a large pan of boiling salted water for 10 minutes until tender but al dente. Drain thoroughly.

Meanwhile, melt the butter in a small pan, add the mushrooms and sauté for 3 minutes. Drain on absorbent kitchen paper. While still warm, mix the pasta with the mussels, prawns and anchovies. Add the mushrooms and tomatoes and pour over the dressing. Mix thoroughly and turn into a serving dish. Chill for 2 hours.

■ COOK'S TIP

In some parts of Italy, this dish is eaten cold. Instead of marinating it before frying, it is fried in the same way as the recipe. A marinade is made in the same way as before but with an extra 150 ml/5 fl oz white wine vinegar and no onion. It is brought to the boil, poured over the fish and left overnight or until cold before it is eaten.

■ COOK'S TIP

Just before serving this salad, sprinkle with 2 tablespoons chopped parsley and 2 tablespoons grated Parmesan cheese, and garnish with 4 lemon twists.

35 MARINATED MACKEREL WITH HERBS

Preparation time:
10 minutes, plus
cooling and
marinating

Cooking time:
12 minutes

Serves 4

Calories:
580 per portion

YOU WILL NEED:
4 mackerel, each weighing about
  225 g/8 oz, cleaned
250 ml/8 fl oz white wine vinegar
salt and pepper
150 ml/¼ pint olive oil
3 garlic cloves, crushed
1 tablespoon chopped parsley
6 mint leaves, chopped
mint sprigs, to garnish

Lay the fish in a large frying pan and pour over just enough water to cover. Bring slowly to the boil, cover and simmer gently for 10 minutes. Drain and leave to cool.

Divide each mackerel into four fillets, discarding the skin. Place in a shallow dish, pour over the vinegar and sprinkle with a little salt and pepper. Leave to marinate for 30 minutes.

Mix the remaining ingredients with a pinch of salt. Drain the mackerel, then return to the dish and pour over the oil marinade. Leave to marinate for a further hour, then drain off the oil. Serve cold, garnished with mint.

■ COOK'S TIP

This is a pleasant dish to serve at a summer lunch or supper in the garden. If liked, add lemon wedges to the garnish.

36 NEAPOLITAN SCAMPI

Preparation time:
25 minutes

Cooking time:
40-45 minutes

Serves 4

Calories:
468 per portion

YOU WILL NEED:
50 g/2 oz seasoned plain flour
450 g/1 lb scampi
25 g/1 oz butter
100 g/4 oz mushrooms, sliced
225 g/8 oz tomatoes, skinned, seeded
  and diced
150 ml/¼ pint double cream
FOR THE SAUCE
150 ml/¼ pint dry white wine
1 small onion, finely chopped
1 bouquet garni
25 g/1 oz butter
25 g/1 oz plain flour
1 garlic clove, crushed
2 teaspoons tomato purée
300 ml/½ pint chicken stock
salt and pepper

Make the sauce: pour the wine, onion and bouquet garni into a small pan, bring to the boil, and reduce to half. Set aside. Melt the butter, stir in the flour and cook 2 minutes. Stir in the remaining ingredients, bring to the boil, and simmer for 15 minutes. Discard the bouquet garni and stir the wine mixture into the sauce mixture. Simmer for a further 10 minutes.

Coat the scampi in the seasoned flour. Melt the butter in a frying pan and sauté the fish gently for about 5 minutes. Transfer to a warm serving dish. Add the mushrooms to the pan and cook 2 minutes. Stir in the sauce, tomatoes and cream, adjust seasoning, bring to the boil and pour over the fish.

■ COOK'S TIP

This dish should be served very hot. Buttered noodles are the traditional accompaniment but plain boiled ones are better with the creamy mixture.

37   SEA BASS BAKED WITH MINT

Preparation time:
20 minutes

Cooking time:
40-45 minutes

Oven temperature:
180 C/350 F/gas 4

Serves 4

Calories:
452 per portion

YOU WILL NEED:
2 × 750 g/1 ½ lb sea bass, cleaned and
  scaled
salt and pepper
olive oil, for brushing
300 ml/½ pint dry white wine
FOR THE STUFFING
bunch of mint leaves
50 g/2 oz softened butter
100 g/4 oz white breadcrumbs
4 tablespoons lemon juice
salt and pepper
bed of mint leaves
quartered lemon slices

Wash the two sea bass and dry with absorbent kitchen paper. Sprinkle inside and out with salt and pepper.

Chop 4 tablespoons mint leaves and mix with the butter, breadcrumbs, lemon juice, salt and pepper. Stuff the fish cavities with this mixture.

Place the fish in a baking dish and brush with olive oil. Arrange mint leaves, overlapping, to cover the fish. Pour on the wine and cover with foil.

Bake in a preheated oven for 40-45 minutes until the fish is tender. Arrange on a bed of mint leaves and put a line of lemon slices down the centre of each fish.

38   FISHERMAN'S SAUCE

Preparation time:
20 minutes

Cooking time:
1 hour

Serves 4

Calories:
722 per portion

YOU WILL NEED:
1 × 400 g/14 oz can tomatoes
400 g/14 oz mixed, cleaned and shelled
  molluscs and shellfish (for example,
  prawns, clams, mussels, squid, baby
  octopus, cuttlefish)
olive oil
2 garlic cloves, cut into 3-4 pieces
1 small chilli
salt
350 g/12 oz linguine
small bunch of parsley, roughly
  chopped

Crush the tomatoes or blend them briefly in a liquidizer. Cut the squid, cuttlefish and octopus into small pieces.

Cover the bottom of a large frying pan with olive oil. When the oil is hot, but not smoking, add the garlic and chilli. Fry the garlic until golden and crush the chilli against the bottom of the pan to release its flavour. Add the pieces of squid, cuttlefish and octopus to the hot oil and fry, stirring contents for about 5-6 minutes. Add the tomatoes and salt to taste and simmer gently for about 30 minutes, adding the mussels, clams and prawns 10 minutes before the sauce is ready. While cooking, stir the sauce occasionally and add a little water if necessary to prevent it sticking. When the pasta is cooked, transfer it to a serving dish, add the chopped parsley and pour the hot sauce over the top.

Serve garnished with more chopped parsley and a few mussel and clam shells if available.

■ COOK'S TIP

If sea bass is not available, grey mullet or hake can be used instead. Soak grey mullet overnight in salted water before cooking.

■ COOK'S TIP

The above sauce can also be served without the addition of tomatoes. It can also be made with cream. In this case the sauce should be liquidized and the cream

added. You will only need half the ingredients given above plus 150 ml/¼ pint single cream.

39 GREY MULLET WITH COURGETTES

Preparation time:
20 minutes plus
draining time

Cooking time:
45-50 minutes

Oven temperature:
190 C/375 F/gas 5

Serves 4-5

Calories:
712-569 per portion

YOU WILL NEED:
salt and pepper
450 g/1 lb courgettes, trimmed and
*   sliced*
150 ml/5 fl oz olive oil
1 large onion, chopped
2 garlic cloves, crushed
3 tablespoons chopped parsley
1 × 1-1.5 kg/2-2 ½ lb grey mullet,
*   gutted, scaled and trimmed*
4 tablespoons lemon juice

Prepare the courgettes (see Cook's Tip). Heat 2 tablespoons oil in a pan and cook the onion and garlic until soft but without colour. Add the courgettes and 2 tablespoons chopped parsley and season if necessary.

Wash the fish and season it inside and out with salt and pepper. Place the fish in a large ovenproof dish, spoon the courgette mixture around the fish and pour over the rest of the oil and the lemon juice. Cover with a lid or aluminium foil and cook in a preheated oven for 20 minutes. Spoon some of the cooking liquor over the fish. Cook uncovered for a further 15 minutes or until the fish is tender, basting the fish and courgettes with the cooking liquor once or twice.

Carefully transfer the fish to a hot serving dish, spoon the courgettes around the side and pour the cooking liquor over. Sprinkle the remaining parsley over and serve hot.

■ COOK'S TIP

Sprinkle 1 teaspoon salt over the sliced courgettes and leave in a colander or on a wire cooling tray to drain for 30 minutes. Rinse under the cold tap and drain again, *then dry on absorbent kitchen paper.*

40 MARINATED SCAMPI KEBABS

Preparation time:
15 minutes, plus
marinating

Cooking time:
5-8 minutes

Serves 4

Calories:
313 per portion

YOU WILL NEED:
450 g/1 lb scampi
FOR THE MARINADE
2 garlic cloves, crushed
4 tablespoons olive oil
3 tablespoons chopped parsley
4 teaspoons lemon juice
50 g/2 oz dry white breadcrumbs
salt and pepper
bay leaves

Rinse the scampi and dry well with absorbent kitchen paper. Mix together the garlic, oil, parsley, lemon juice, breadcrumbs, salt and pepper. Add the scampi and mix well. Leave to marinate for a minimum of 1 hour.

Thread the scampi on to four skewers, with an occasional bay leaf between. Place under a preheated moderate grill, turning occasionally until golden and crispy.

■ COOK'S TIP

Plain boiled rice or a risotto with mushrooms makes a good accompaniment to the scampi, with a crisp green side salad. Drink either a dry white or a light red wine.

41 MIXED FRIED SEA FOOD

Preparation time:
30-40 minutes

Cooking time:
15-20 minutes

Serves 4

Calories:
386 per portion

YOU WILL NEED:
100-175 g/4-6 oz prepared squid, sliced
100-175 g/4-6 oz whitebait
100-175 g/4-6 oz large prawns
100-175 g/4-6 oz plaice fillets, skinned
  and cut into 1 cm/ ½ inch strips
100 g/4 oz plain flour
salt and pepper
oil for deep frying
1-2 lemons, sliced or quartered

Wash all the fish and dry well. Season the flour well with salt and pepper. Heat the oil in a deep pan to 180-190 C/350-375 F or until a cube of bread browns in 30 seconds. Toss the fish, a batch at a time, into the seasoned flour and fry until golden brown. Drain well on absorbent kitchen paper, place on a hot serving dish and keep hot. Just before serving, sprinkle the fish lightly with salt and garnish the dish with the lemon.

42 BAKED STUFFED SQUID

Preparation time:
30-35 minutes

Cooking time:
1¼ hours

Oven temperature:
180 C/350 F/gas 4

Serves 4

Calories:
261 per portion

YOU WILL NEED:
800 g/1 ¾ lb squid
salt
4 canned anchovies, mashed
1 garlic clove, crushed
1 tablespoon dried breadcrumbs
1 tablespoon chopped parsley
1 egg, beaten
3 tablespoons olive oil
fennel leaves, to garnish

Clean the squid, discarding the heads, inksacs and backbones. Cut off the tentacles and set aside the squid. Cook the tentacles in boiling salted water for 10 minutes. Drain, chop and place in a bowl. Add the remaining ingredients, except the oil, seasoning with salt and pepper to taste.

Stuff the squid with this mixture, and sew up the opening with thread. Place the squid in an ovenproof dish and sprinkle with the oil.

Bake in a preheated oven for 1 hour or until tender. Serve immediately, garnished with fennel.

■ COOK'S TIP

Any selection of small fish or pieces of fish can be used in this dish, such as queen scallops, pieces of skate or monkfish, cooked shelled mussels, small peeled prawns, *sprats or smelts. The quantities given are a guide only. You may prefer more or less of one type of fish.*

■ COOK'S TIP

Use white cotton thread and a darning needle to sew up the squid. Leave sufficiently long ends for the thread to be removed easily before serving.

43 RED MULLET WITH TOMATOES

Preparation time:
15-20 minutes

Cooking time:
30-35 minutes

Serves 4

Calories:
417 per portion

YOU WILL NEED:
6-8 tablespoons olive oil
1 onion, finely chopped
1 garlic clove, crushed
2-3 anchovy fillets, chopped
1 × 400 g/14 oz can chopped tomatoes
150 ml/5 fl oz dry white wine
1 bay leaf
¼ teaspoon chopped thyme
salt and pepper
4 × 225-350 g/8-12 oz red mullet, scales
   and fins removed
4 tablespoons seasoned plain flour
12 black olives, pitted
1 tablespoon chopped parsley

Heat 2 tablespoons oil in a pan and cook the onion and garlic gently until lightly coloured. Add the anchovy fillets, tomatoes, white wine, bay leaf and thyme. Season to taste and cook gently for about 20 minutes until the sauce thickens.

Meanwhile, heat 4-6 tablespoons of the oil in a frying pan. Coat the fish with the flour. Fry until golden brown on one side, then turn carefully and cook on the second side.

When the sauce is ready, add to the pan with the red mullet and cook for a further 6-8 minutes. Transfer the fish carefully to a hot serving dish. Toss the olives in the sauce and heat through. Remove the bay leaf and pour the sauce over the fish. Sprinkle the parsley over and serve hot.

44 BABY CLAM SAUCE

Preparation time:
15 minutes, plus
standing

Cooking time:
about 15 minutes

Serves 4

Calories:
415 per portion

YOU WILL NEED:
450 g/1 lb fresh baby clams, in their
   shells
olive oil
3 garlic cloves, cut into 3-4 pieces
small bunch of parsley, roughly
   chopped
pepper
350 g/12 oz spaghetti

Put the clams in a bowl of water and leave for 2-3 hours to allow them to expel any sand in their shells. Wash the clams thoroughly by rubbing the shells together between your hands under running water.

Thickly coat the bottom of a very large pan with olive oil. Add the garlic and fry gently until golden. Add the clams and cover the pan. The heat of the oil and the pan will force the clams to open and they will cook in their own juice. Stir the clams occasionally until all of the shells are open. This should take about 10 minutes. The clams will release sea water so it should not be necessary to add salt.

Take half of the clams out of their shells, putting them back in the saucepan and discarding the shells. Add pepper and chopped parsley. Keep the sauce hot while cooking the spaghetti. When the pasta is cooked, transfer it to a serving dish and pour the sauce over the top.

■ COOK'S TIP

When scraping the scales from the fish, work from the tail to the head then cut off the fins with a pair of kitchen scissors. Red mullet are usually cooked ungutted

as it is thought that the fish gains flavour from the guts and the liver is considered a delicacy.

■ COOK'S TIP

If any of the clams do not open when cooked, discard them. You may prefer to remove most of the shells before serving but keep some for garnish.

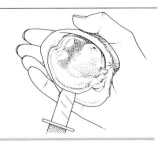

45 PRAWNS IN A CREAM SAUCE

Preparation time:
10-15 minutes

Cooking time:
10-15 minutes

Serves 4

Calories:
439 per portion

YOU WILL NEED:
50 g/2 oz butter
24 king-sized uncooked prawns, shelled
2 tablespoons brandy
225 ml/7 ½ fl oz double cream
2-3 teaspoons French mustard
salt and white pepper
chopped parsley

Heat the butter in a frying pan and cook the prawns for a few moments. Warm the brandy, pour over the prawns and set alight. When the flames have subsided, stir in the cream. Season to taste with the mustard, salt and white pepper. Simmer very gently (to prevent the prawns toughening) for 4-5 minutes until the prawns are tender. Pour into a hot serving dish and sprinkle chopped parsley over just before serving. Serve with boiled rice or tagliatelle.

46 FRESH TUNA WITH TOMATOES

Preparation time:
15 minutes, plus standing

Cooking time:
about 35 minutes

Serves 4

Calories:
423 per portion

YOU WILL NEED:
4 tuna steaks
salt and pepper
flour for dusting
3 tablespoons olive oil
1 small onion, chopped
1 garlic clove, crushed
750 g/1 ½ lb tomatoes, skinned and chopped
2 tablespoons chopped parsley
1 bay leaf
4 anchovy fillets, mashed
6 black olives

Season the fish with salt and pepper and dust with flour. Heat half the oil in a large shallow frying pan. Sauté the fish quickly until golden on both sides. Carefully transfer to a plate.

Add the remaining oil to the pan, add the onion and garlic and sauté for 5 minutes until soft. Add the tomatoes, parsley, bay leaf and anchovies, and stir for a few seconds. Bring to the boil and continue boiling until the mixture has reduced to a thin sauce. Season with pepper, return the fish to the pan and simmer gently for 15 minutes, turning once. Turn off the heat, add the olives and leave for 5 minutes. Transfer to a warm serving dish and serve immediately.

■ COOK'S TIP

For a less expensive dish, use 450 g/1 lb peeled prawns. In this case, boil the cream first for 4-5 minutes until it thickens slightly. Heat the prawns in the butter, flambé with the brandy, pour the cream over, season to taste with mustard, salt and pepper and serve immediately.

■ COOK'S TIP

Ideally, use an Italian olive oil for cooking the tuna steaks. The best quality is reputed to come from the town of Lucca in Tuscany.

47　DEEP-FRIED ANCHOVIES

Preparation time:
20 minutes

Cooking time:
about 10 minutes

Serves 4

Calories:
579 per portion

YOU WILL NEED:
575 g/1¼ lb fresh anchovies
2 eggs, beaten with a pinch of salt
about 200 g/7 oz dry white
　breadcrumbs
vegetable oil for deep-frying
salt
lemon slices, to serve

Slit the anchovies along one side, clean thoroughly and remove the heads and backbones. Press each anchovy flat, then combine them in pairs with their open sides face to face. Press firmly so that they adhere to each other.

Dip each pair of anchovies in the beaten egg, then coat with breadcrumbs. Heat the oil in a deep-fryer and deep-fry the anchovies until golden brown. Drain on absorbent kitchen paper, then sprinkle with salt. Serve immediately, with lemon slices.

48　SALMON CASSEROLE

Preparation time:
about 20 minutes,
plus soaking

Cooking time:
40-45 minutes

Oven temperature:
180 C/350 F/gas 4

Serves 4

Calories:
556 per portion

YOU WILL NEED:
4 salmon steaks, each 175 g/6 oz
plain flour for coating
4 tablespoons olive oil
salt and pepper
1 small onion, chopped
1 celery stick, chopped
2 garlic cloves, crushed
450 g/1 lb tomatoes, skinned and
　mashed
25 g/1 oz seedless raisins, soaked in
　lukewarm water for 15 minutes and
　drained
25 g/1 oz pine nuts
1 tablespoon capers
100 g/4 oz green olives, halved and
　stoned
2 bay leaves

Coat the fish with flour. Heat the oil in a flameproof casserole, add the fish and fry until golden brown on both sides. Remove and drain on absorbent kitchen paper, then sprinkle with salt and pepper.

Add the onion, celery and garlic to the casserole and fry gently for 5 minutes. Add the tomatoes, with salt and pepper to taste, and simmer for 15 minutes. Stir in the raisins, pine nuts, capers and olives, and cook for 5 minutes.

Return the fish to the casserole, add the bay leaves and enough water to just cover the fish. Cover and cook in a preheated oven for 15-20 minutes until the fish is tender.

■ COOK'S TIP

The Italians are fortunate to have plentiful supplies of fresh anchovies, but these are not so common outside Italy. Small fresh sardines can be used as a substitute, or even smelts or sprats when they are available.

■ COOK'S TIP

Swordfish steaks may be used in this casserole instead of salmon. They have a slightly stronger flavour and are rather more expensive.

49 DEEP-FRIED SARDINES WITH CHEESE STUFFING

Preparation time:
30 minutes, plus marinating

Cooking time:
15-20 minutes

Serves 6

Calories:
489 per portion

YOU WILL NEED:
800 g/1 ¾ lb fresh sardines
200 ml/7 fl oz white wine vinegar
75 g/3 oz pecorino cheese, grated
3 garlic cloves, crushed
1 tablespoon chopped parsley or basil
salt and pepper
2 eggs, beaten
dry white breadcrumbs for coating
vegetable oil for shallow-frying
basil or parsley sprigs, to garnish

Slit the sardines open along one side and clean thoroughly, removing the backbones but leaving the heads and tails intact. Open the fish out and place in a shallow bowl. Pour over the vinegar and leave to marinate for 2 hours turning occasionally.

Drain the sardines. Mix the pecorino, garlic and parsley with salt and pepper to taste. Spread this mixture over the insides of the sardines and fold to close. Dip the sardines in the eggs and coat with breadcrumbs.

Pour the oil into a frying pan to a depth of 5 mm/¼ inch and place over moderate heat. Fry the sardines until brown on both sides. Drain on absorbent kitchen paper and serve immediately, garnished with basil or parsley sprigs.

50 FRESH TUNA WITH MUSHROOMS

Preparation time:
15-20 minutes

Cooking time:
55-60 minutes

Oven temperature:
190 C/375 F/gas 5

Serves 4

Calories:
543 per portion

YOU WILL NEED:
4-6 tablespoons oil
2-3 garlic cloves, crushed
1 large onion, finely chopped
150 g/5 oz button mushrooms,
    quartered or thickly sliced
6-8 anchovy fillets, chopped
2 tablespoons chopped parsley
1 tablespoon plain flour
300 ml/10 fl oz dry white wine
pepper
pinch nutmeg
4 × 150-225 g/6-8 oz tuna steaks about
    1 cm/½ inch thick

Heat the oil in a pan and cook the garlic and onion until it is soft and lightly coloured. Add the mushrooms and cook for 2-3 minutes, then add the anchovies, parsley and flour. Mix well together. Stir in the wine, bring to the boil, stirring all the time, then simmer for 5-7 minutes. Season to taste with pepper and a pinch of nutmeg. There should be no need to add salt because the anchovies are salty.

Place the tuna steaks in an oven-to-table dish and pour the sauce over. Cover with a lid or foil and cook in a preheated oven for 40-45 minutes. Serve hot. If you wish, a tomato sauce, such as that in recipe 81, can be served with this dish.

■ COOK'S TIP

Home-made dry breadcrumbs are better than bought ones. Toast thin slices of bread, put into a plastic bag and crush with a rolling pin. Alternatively, use a blender.

■ COOK'S TIP

Swordfish or halibut steaks could also be used in this recipe, in place of the tuna.

51　SHRIMPS WITH HERBS

Preparation time:
10 minutes

Cooking time:
5-7 minutes

Serves 4

Calories:
292 per portion

YOU WILL NEED:
4 tablespoons olive oil
4 garlic cloves
575 g/1 ¼ lb peeled, cooked shrimps
5 basil leaves, finely chopped
5 marjoram leaves, finely chopped
3-4 parsley sprigs, finely chopped
pinch of paprika
pinch of salt
3-4 tablespoons dry white wine
marjoram sprigs, to garnish

Heat the oil in a flameproof casserole, add the garlic cloves and fry gently until browned. Remove the garlic, then add the shrimps, herbs, paprika, salt and wine and cook gently until the shrimps are heated through.

Serve immediately, garnished with marjoram.

52　DEEP-FRIED PAPRIKA SARDINES

Preparation time:
10 minutes

Cooking time:
3-4 minutes

Serves 4

Calories:
380 per portion

YOU WILL NEED:
450 g/1 lb fresh or frozen sardines,
　thawed if frozen
1 teaspoon salt
4 teaspoons paprika
4 teaspoons plain flour
oil, for deep frying
FOR THE GARNISH
lemon slices
sprigs of parsley

Clean the sardines if necessary, wash inside and out and pat dry with absorbent kitchen paper.

Sift the salt, paprika and flour on to a plate. Roll the sardines in this mixture until well coated.

Heat the oil to 180 C/350 F or until a cube of bread browns in 30 seconds. Fry the sardines for 3-4 minutes until crispy and golden. Drain on absorbent kitchen paper and serve with the lemon slices, garnished with parsley.

■ COOK'S TIP

Shrimps cooked in this way can be served as a starter, in which case the quantity would be sufficient for 6. As a main course, serve with pasta or plain boiled rice.

■ COOK'S TIP

Fry the sardines in batches. Too many sardines in the pan at once will lower the oil temperature, and the fish batter will become soggy.

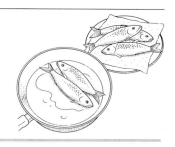

PASTA

There are over one hundred different forms of pasta on the market in Italy. With the increasing popularity of pasta in this country, many more varieties – both fresh and dried – are now available. You can also make pasta dough quite easily. The recipes in this chapter have been chosen to show the versatility of pasta.

53 PENNE WITH CHILLI SAUCE

Preparation time:
10-15 minutes

Cooking time:
40-50 minutes

Serves 4

Calories:
591 per portion

YOU WILL NEED:
1-2 tablespoons olive oil
1 large onion, finely chopped
2 garlic cloves, crushed
100 g/4 oz rindless streaky bacon,
chopped
1-2 fresh red chillies, chopped
1 × 400 g/14 oz can chopped tomatoes
50-75 g/2-3 oz Pecorino or Parmesan
cheese, grated
salt and pepper
450 g/1 lb penne

Heat the oil in a pan and cook the onion, garlic and bacon until they are lightly coloured. Add the chillies, tomatoes and 25 g/1 oz of the cheese. Season to taste with salt and pepper and cook over a gentle heat for 30-40 minutes until the sauce thickens. Check the seasoning.

Cook the penne in boiling, salted water for about 12 minutes until just tender (al dente). Drain well and place in a hot serving dish. Stir in most of the sauce, mix well and then pour the remainder of the sauce over the top. Serve the remainder of the cheese separately.

54 EGG PASTA DOUGH

Preparation time:
15-20 minutes, plus resting and rolling the dough

Makes 450 g/1 lb

Total calories:
1,884

YOU WILL NEED:
450 g/1 lb plain flour
good pinch of salt
2 large or 3 medium eggs
1 teaspoon oil
3-4 tablespoons water

Sift the flour and salt into a bowl. Make a hollow in the centre and drop in the eggs and oil. Draw the flour into the centre, add 3 tablespoons water and knead well; add another tablespoon of water if the mixture is too dry. Knead the dough until smooth and very elastic; this is essential, if the dough is to roll properly. Wrap the dough in clingfilm and leave to rest for a minimum of 15 minutes and a maximum of 2 hours.

Working quickly, flatten the dough with the rolling pin, giving the dough a quarter turn between each roll, until it measures 20-23 cm/8-9 inches in diameter.

Hold the near edge of the dough down with one hand and place the rolling pin on the opposite edge. Curl the end of the dough around the rolling pin and push with the pin to stretch the dough. Keep moving the pin towards you along the dough, stopping, stretching the dough, then rolling up more dough, until you have taken up all the dough. Give the pin a quarter turn so that it points towards you and unfurl the sheet of dough, opening it up flat. Repeat the rolling and stretching until the dough has been stretched to a square measuring about 40-45 cm/16-18 inches. Roll out the dough until it is paper thin, then use as required.

■ COOK'S TIP

You can buy both red and green chillies, the red ones being hotter. For a milder taste, slice the chillies in half lengthways and scrape out the seeds with the point of a small knife before chopping them. Be careful not to touch your eyes or mouth and wash your hands well after handling chillies as the juice is very pungent.

■ COOK'S TIP

Although hand rolling is best for pasta, a pasta machine makes the job easier and quicker. Either way, practice is essential.

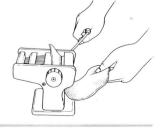

55 GREEN PASTA DOUGH

Preparation time:
25 minutes, plus
resting

Cooking time:
about 5 minutes

Makes 450 g/1 lb

Total calories:
1,688

YOU WILL NEED:
300 g/11 oz frozen whole-leaf spinach
400 g/14 oz strong plain flour
2 eggs
1 egg yolk

Cook the spinach in boiling salted water and drain well, squeezing out as much water as possible until the spinach looks quite dry. Chop it finely until it has almost become a 'paste'.

Heap the flour on a working surface and make a deep well in the centre. Break the eggs into the well, add the yolk and, using a fork, lightly beat the eggs. Add the chopped spinach a little at a time while beating the flour into the eggs.

Continue as for Egg pasta dough (recipe 54). Green pasta is slightly moister than plain pasta so remember to flour the working surface well before rolling out the dough.

■ COOK'S TIP

Red-coloured pasta can be obtained by adding tomato purée instead of the spinach. Yellow-coloured pasta can be made by adding saffron.

56 FETTUCCINE WITH BOLOGNESE SAUCE

Preparation time:
20 minutes

Cooking time:
about 55 minutes

Serves 4

Calories:
623 per portion

YOU WILL NEED:
575 g/1 ¼ lb canned tomatoes
olive oil
1 garlic clove, halved
1 onion, finely chopped
1 carrot, finely chopped
1 celery stick, finely chopped
150 g/5 oz lean minced beef
150 ml/ ¼ pint dry white wine
1 tablespoon tomato purée
salt
450 g/1 lb fettuccine
butter and Parmesan cheese, to serve

Crush the tomatoes or blend them briefly in a liquidizer. Coat the bottom of a saucepan with olive oil. Fry the garlic until golden, add the onion, carrot and celery and fry gently until the onion is transparent and the carrot and celery are softer. Stirring constantly, add the minced beef and fry until it has browned. Add the wine and when it has evaporated, add the tomato purée and tomatoes. Add salt to taste and simmer gently for about 45 minutes, adding a little water if the sauce sticks to the pan. When ready the sauce should be dense and dark in colour.

Meanwhile, cook the fettuccine in boiling, salted water until just tender (al dente). Drain, transfer to a serving dish and pour the sauce over the top. Serve individual portions with a knob of butter and grated Parmesan cheese.

■ COOK'S TIP

It is best to make this sauce well in advance, even the day before serving. Chopped mushrooms may be added with the other vegetables, if liked.

57 BAKED LASAGNE

Preparation time:
20 minutes

Cooking time:
40-45 minutes plus
time for making
sauces

Oven temperature:
180 C/350 F/gas 4

Serves 4

Calories:
868 per portion

YOU WILL NEED:
150-300 ml/ ¼- ½ pint milk
*450 ml/15 fl oz Béchamel Sauce (see
    Cook's Tip)*
salt and white pepper
*1 × quantity Bolognese sauce (recipe
    56) cooked for 20 minutes only*
*225 g/8 oz ready-to-cook green or
    white lasagne or fresh pasta cut into
    thin 19 × 9 cm (7½ × 3½ inch)
    sheets*
*350 g/12 oz Bel Paese or Fontina
    cheese, thinly sliced or grated*
*2-3 tablespoons Parmesan cheese,
    grated*

Whisk sufficient milk into the Béchamel sauce to adjust it to a
thin creamy consistency. Check the seasoning. Butter an oven-
to-table dish and, starting with a little Bolognese sauce, layer
the Bolognese sauce, lasagne, Béchamel sauce and Bel Paese or
Fontina cheese in the dish, ending with a layer of Béchamel
sauce. Sprinkle the Parmesan cheese over the top and bake in a
preheated oven for 40-45 minutes. Serve hot.

58 CHEESE-FILLED RAVIOLI

Preparation time:
30-35 minutes, plus
standing

Cooking time:
about 5 minutes

Serves 4

Calories:
973 per portion

YOU WILL NEED:
400 g/14 oz plain flour
salt
4 eggs, beaten
1.5 litres/2 ½ pints stock
100 g/4 oz butter, melted
75 g/3 oz Parmesan cheese, grated
FOR THE FILLING
225 g/8 oz ricotta cheese
100 g/4 oz Bel Paese cheese, grated
50 g/2 oz Parmesan cheese, grated
2 eggs, beaten
pinch of grated nutmeg

To make the pasta sift the flour and a pinch of salt on to a
work surface and make a well in the centre. Add the eggs and
mix to a smooth dough. Shape into a ball, wrap in a damp
cloth and leave for about 30 minutes.

Meanwhile, make the filling: put the ricotta and Bel Paese
in a bowl and beat well. Add the remaining ingredients with a
pinch of salt and beat thoroughly.

Roll out the dough paper-thin. Cut into 4 cm/1¾ inch
squares with a tooth-edged rotary cutter. Put a little filling in
the centre of each square, then fold the dough over to make
triangles. Turn the corners upwards. Bring the stock to the boil
in a large pan. Add the ravioli and cook for 5 minutes or until
they rise to the surface. Remove with a slotted spoon and pile
into a warmed serving dish. Sprinkle with the melted butter
and Parmesan and serve immediately.

■ COOK'S TIP

*Béchamel sauce: melt 40 g/
1½ oz butter, add 40 g/1½ oz
flour and cook 2-3 minutes.
Slowly add 450 ml/15 fl oz
milk, stirring. Bring slowly to
the boil, stirring, then let*
*sauce boil gently for 2-3
minutes. Season with salt,
pepper and a little nutmeg.*

■ COOK'S TIP

*Strain the stock after cooking
the ravioli and use to make
soup for another meal. The
ravioli can be cooked in
salted water if no stock is
available.*

59 FRIED RAVIOLI

Preparation time:
30-35 minutes

Cooking time:
about 10 minutes

Serves 6

Calories:
441 per portion

YOU WILL NEED:
300 g/11 oz plain flour
salt and pepper
50 g/2 oz butter, diced
2 egg yolks
1 egg white, lightly whisked
vegetable oil for deep-frying
FOR THE FILLING
100 g/4 oz gruyère cheese, diced
75 g/3 oz cooked ham, minced
40 g/1 ½ oz Parmesan cheese, grated
1 egg beaten
1 tablespoon chopped parsley

Sift the flour and a pinch of salt on to a work surface and make a well in the centre. Add the butter and egg yolks and work to a smooth dough, adding a little lukewarm water if necessary.

To make the filling, put the ingredients in a bowl with salt and pepper. Stir well until thoroughly combined.

Flatten the dough with a rolling pin and roll out to a sheet about 5 mm/¼ inch thick. Cut into 12.5 cm/5 inch circles. Divide the filling between the circles, placing it in the centre of each one. Brush the edges of the circles with a little egg white, then fold the dough over the filling to enclose it completely. Deep-fry the ravioli a few at a time in hot oil until golden brown. Drain on absorbent kitchen paper. Serve hot.

60 PESARO-STYLE ZITONE

Preparation time:
20-25 minutes

Cooking time:
about 35 minutes

Oven temperature:
200 C/400 F/gas 6

Serves 4

Calories:
745 per portion

YOU WILL NEED:
175 g/6 oz turkey breast meat
2 chicken livers
100 g/4 oz ham
50 g/2 oz mushrooms
100 g/4 oz butter
1 small onion, chopped
7 tablespoons dry white wine
pinch of grated nutmeg
salt and pepper
1 tablespoon single cream
300 g/11 oz zitone
75 g/3 oz gruyère cheese, grated

Mince the turkey, chicken livers, ham and mushrooms. Melt 2 tablespoons of the butter in a heavy pan, add the onion and fry gently until golden. Stir in the minced mixture and cook, stirring for 10 minutes. Add the wine and simmer gently until it has evaporated by half, then add the nutmeg with salt and pepper to taste. Transfer to a bowl, add a little of the cream and stir well, to give a smooth, creamy filling.

Meanwhile cook the zitone in boiling, salted water until just tender (al dente). Drain thoroughly, then stuff with the filling and arrange in two layers in a buttered baking dish, covering each layer with the remaining cream and gruyère. Dot the remaining butter over the top. Bake in a preheated oven for 15 minutes until golden brown.

■ COOK'S TIP

Try making miniature versions of the ravioli to serve as hot canapés at a drinks party. Cut the dough into 3.5 cm/1 ½ inch circles.

■ COOK'S TIP

Turkey breast meat is now available all the year in major supermarkets. If preferred, boneless chicken fillets could be used instead in this recipe.

61 TRENETTE WITH ANCHOVIES

Preparation time:
20-30 minutes

Cooking time:
20-25 minutes

Serves 4

Calories:
708 per portion

YOU WILL NEED:

4-6 tablespoons olive oil

2 garlic cloves, crushed

2 large onions, finely chopped

1 red pepper, skinned, seeded and cut
   into strips

1 yellow pepper, skinned, seeded and
   cut into strips

1 × 400 g/14 oz can plum tomatoes,
   drained, seeded and chopped

1 × 40 g/1½ oz can anchovies, drained
   and chopped

pepper

pinch sugar

450 g/1 lb trenette

8 tablespoons Parmesan cheese, grated

1 tablespoon chopped parsley

Heat half the oil in a pan and cook the garlic and onions until soft and just beginning to colour. Add the peppers and cook until soft, add the tomatoes and anchovies, season with pepper and stir in the sugar. Cook a few minutes longer until the tomatoes and anchovies are heated through.

Meanwhile, cook the trenette in boiling salted water for about 7 minutes until just tender (al dente). Drain well. Place in a hot serving dish and stir in a little sauce, half the cheese and, if you wish, the remainder of the oil. Just before serving, pour the rest of the sauce over and sprinkle the chopped parsley over the top. Serve hot with the rest of the cheese served separately.

62 TUNA FISH SAUCE

Preparation time:
10 minutes

Cooking time:
15-20 minutes

Serves 4

Calories:
104 per portion
(sauce only)

YOU WILL NEED:

575 g/1¼ lb canned tomatoes

2 garlic cloves, each cut into 3-4 pieces

small bunch of parsley, roughly
   chopped

olive oil

salt and pepper

1 × 200 g/7 oz can tuna, drained and
   flaked

Start making the sauce before cooking the chosen pasta. Crush the tomatoes or blend them briefly in a liquidizer. Coat the bottom of a large frying pan with olive oil and when it is hot, but not smoking, add the garlic and fry gently until golden. Add the tomatoes, season to taste and simmer gently for about 10-15 minutes. Add the tuna.

When the chosen pasta is cooked, transfer it to a serving dish and pour the sauce over the top. Serve individual portions garnished with the chopped parsley.

■ COOK'S TIP

To remove the skins from the peppers, place the halved or quartered peppers under a moderately hot grill until the skins start to char and curl. Scrape the skins off.

■ COOK'S TIP

Spaghetti or linguine are a good choice of pasta for this dish. The tuna fish sauce should be ready just as you are draining the pasta.

63 SPAGHETTI ALLA CARBONARA

Preparation time:
10 minutes

Cooking time:
5 minutes (for the sauce)

Serves 4

Calories:
740 per portion

YOU WILL NEED:
450 g/1 lb spaghetti
4 eggs
50 g/2 oz pecorino cheese, grated
50 g/2 oz Parmesan cheese, grated
salt and pepper
4 rindless rashers lean streaky bacon
3 tablespoons olive oil

Put the pasta in boiling, lightly salted water to cook, then prepare the sauce.

Lightly beat the eggs with a fork in a bowl, adding half the grated cheese and seasoning to taste. Cut the bacon into small squares of about 1 cm/½ inch.

Gently fry the bacon in the olive oil until it becomes crispy. Turn off the heat. While draining the freshly cooked pasta, turn on the heat under the bacon so that the oil is really hot. As soon as the pasta has been thoroughly drained, put it back in the hot pan it was cooked in and, stirring all the time, pour in the beaten egg and then the bacon and olive oil. On contact with the hot pasta the egg will start to cook and the addition of the boiling oil and bacon turns the egg into a thick creamy sauce which coats the spaghetti.

Serve immediately as the egg will continue to cook for some time and will eventually become too thick and turn the spaghetti into a solid mass! Serve with the remaining mixed grated cheese served separately.

■ COOK'S TIP

This sauce takes practice to make perfectly. Should the egg not cook sufficiently on contact with the pasta and oil, put the pan over the heat for a minute, but stir constantly to prevent scrambled egg forming in the bottom of the pan.

64 VERMICELLI SYRACUSE-STYLE

Preparation time:
25 minutes, plus soaking

Cooking time:
about 25 minutes

Serves 4

Calories:
605 per portion

YOU WILL NEED:
7 tablespoons olive oil
2 garlic cloves
1 aubergine, diced
400 g/14 oz tomatoes, skinned and mashed
1 green pepper (see Cook's Tip)
1 tablespoon capers
8 black olives, halved and stoned
1 tablespoon chopped basil
4 canned anchovies, drained and soaked in milk for 30 minutes
pepper
400 g/14 oz vermicelli
75 g/3 oz pecorino cheese, grated

Heat the oil in a heavy pan, add the garlic cloves and fry gently until browned. Discard the garlic. Add the aubergine and tomatoes and simmer for 10 minutes. Add the pepper, capers, olives, basil and anchovies with pepper to taste. Simmer for a further 10 minutes, stirring frequently.

Meanwhile cook the vermicelli in boiling, salted water until just tender (al dente). Drain thoroughly and pile into a warmed serving dish. Pour over the sauce, sprinkle with pecorino and fold gently to mix. Serve immediately.

■ COOK'S TIP

Grill the pepper under a medium grill, turning frequently, until charred. Peel off the skin. Halve the pepper, remove the core and seeds and slice the flesh.

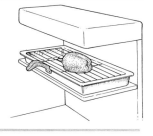

65 PENNE WITH ASPARAGUS SAUCE

Preparation time:
10 minutes

Cooking time:
about 15 minutes

Serves 4

Calories:
788 per portion

YOU WILL NEED:
900 g/2 lb asparagus
salt
100 g/4 oz butter
100 g/4 oz Parmesan cheese, grated
450 g/1 lb penne

Start making the sauce before cooking the penne. Boil the asparagus in salted water until cooked, but not too soft. Discard the stalks, leaving only the green and purple spears. Cut these into 2.5 cm/1 in lengths. Melt the butter in a large frying pan and sauté the asparagus for a few minutes.

Cook the penne in boiling, salted water until just tender (al dente). Drain, transfer it to a serving dish and add the asparagus with the grated Parmesan. Mix well, adding a little of the pasta cooking water if necessary to keep the mixture moist.

Serve immediately with a little more grated Parmesan served separately, if liked.

66 MEAT-FILLED CANNELLONI

Preparation time:
20-30 minutes

Cooking time:
1-1½ hours

Oven temperature:
180 C/350 F/gas 4

Serves 4

Calories:
487 per portion

YOU WILL NEED:
1-2 tablespoons olive oil
350 g/12 oz lean stewing veal, diced
1 onion, sliced
1 carrot, sliced
150 ml/5 fl oz dry white wine
300 ml/10 fl oz chicken stock
salt and pepper
100 g/4 oz cooked chicken
100 g/4 oz cooked spinach, chopped
2-3 tablespoons cream
12 tubes ready-to-cook cannelloni
2 × quantity Tomato sauce (recipe 81)
40 g/1 ½ oz Parmesan cheese, grated

Heat the oil in a pan and fry the veal until it is golden brown. Remove from the pan and add the vegetables and cook until lightly coloured. Return the veal to the pan with the wine and stock. Season lightly and simmer gently for 40-45 minutes until the meat is tender. Remove the meat and vegetables from the pan and mince or chop finely in a food processor with the chicken. Stir in the chopped spinach. Boil the meat stock until it has reduced to about 2 tablespoons. Stir into the meat and spinach mixture with sufficient cream to soften the mixture.

Pipe or spoon the filling into the cannelloni tubes. Place the filled cannelloni in a buttered oven-to-table dish and pour the tomato sauce over. Bake in a preheated oven for 40-45 minutes. Sprinkle a little Parmesan over the top 5-10 minutes before the end of the cooking time and serve the rest separately.

■ COOK'S TIP

Use the discarded stalks for soup. If fresh asparagus is not available then frozen can be used in the same way. If using canned asparagus, just sauté it in the butter.

■ COOK'S TIP

In the Piedmont region of Italy, cannelloni are made with small pancakes filled with a meat mixture similar to the one above coated, before baking, with a

Béchamel sauce and topped with grated Parmesan cheese.

67   PASTA WITH CAULIFLOWER

Preparation time:
10 minutes

Cooking time:
about 15 minutes

Serves 4

Calories:
645 per portion

YOU WILL NEED:
2 litres/3 ½ pints water
salt and pepper
750 g/1 ½ lb cauliflower, divided into
   florets
400 g/14 oz mezze zite or macaroni
7 tablespoons olive oil
25 g/1 oz stale breadcrumbs

Bring the water and a little salt to the boil in a large pan, add the cauliflower and cook for 3 minutes. Add the chosen pasta and cook until just tender (al dente).

Drain the cauliflower and pasta and pile into a warmed serving dish; keep hot. Heat the oil in a small pan, add the breadcrumbs and fry over brisk heat until well browned. Sprinkle over the cauliflower and pasta, add pepper to taste and fold gently to mix. Serve immediately.

■ COOK'S TIP

The breadcrumbs used in this recipe are neither fresh nor dried! They are best made from a loaf of bread that is 3-4 days old.

68   RAVIOLI WITH RICOTTA AND PROVOLONE

Preparation time:
30 minutes

Cooking time:
about 20 minutes

Serves 4

Calories:
885 per portion

YOU WILL NEED:
400 g/14 oz plain flour
salt
100 g/4 oz lard, diced
2 eggs, beaten
juice of 1 lemon
1 egg white, lightly beaten
vegetable oil for deep-frying
FOR THE FILLING
250 g/9 oz ricotta cheese
100 g/4 oz ham, diced
100 g/4 oz provolone cheese, diced
2 egg yolks

Sift the flour and a pinch of salt on to a work surface and make a well in the centre. Add the lard, eggs and lemon juice, then work all the ingredients together into a smooth dough.

To make the filling press the ricotta through a sieve into a bowl. Add the remaining ingredients with salt and pepper to taste. Mix well until thoroughly combined.

Flatten the dough with a rolling pin and roll out into a fairly thin sheet. Cut out four circles, each one about 20 cm/8 inches in diameter. Divide the filling between the circles, placing it in the centre of each one. Brush the edges of the circles with a little egg white, then fold the dough over the filling to enclose it completely. Deep-fry the ravioli one at a time in hot oil until golden brown. Drain on absorbent kitchen paper. Serve hot.

■ COOK'S TIP

Remember to flour your hands and the work surface from time to time when working the dough. Dust the rolling pin with flour too.

69 CANNELLONI WITH SPINACH FILLING

Preparation time:
50 minutes

Cooking time:
about 1 hour

Oven temperature:
180 C/350 F/gas 4

Serves 6

Calories:
954 per portion

YOU WILL NEED:
50 g/2 oz butter
750 g/1 ½ lb cooked spinach, chopped
225 g/8 oz Ricotta cheese, sieved
75 g/3 oz Parmesan cheese, grated
salt and pepper
grated nutmeg
2 large eggs
12 large cannelloni tubes
25 g/1 oz flour
300 ml/ ½ pint milk
4 tablespoons bran cereal

Melt half the butter in a pan, add the spinach and stir well. Remove from the heat. Beat the Ricotta cheese and half the Parmesan into the spinach and season with salt, pepper and nutmeg. Beat in the eggs. Leave to cool.

Cook the cannelloni tubes in boiling, salted water until just tender (al dente). Drain, refresh in cold water, and drain again. Dry thoroughly with absorbent kitchen paper.

Melt the remaining butter in a pan, stir in the flour, and cook for 1 minute. Remove from the heat and gradually stir in the milk. Bring to the boil, season and simmer 5 minutes.

Fill the cannelloni tubes with the spinach mixture and place in a greased, shallow baking dish. Pour over the sauce and sprinkle with the remaining cheese mixed with cereal. Stand the dish on a baking sheet and bake in a preheated oven for 35-40 minutes or until the topping is crusty.

■ COOK'S TIP

The simplest way to fill the cannelloni tubes is to put the spinach mixture into a piping bag, without a nozzle, and squeeze it gently into the cannelloni.

70 CONCHIGLIE WITH CALABRIAN SAUCE

Preparation time:
15 minutes

Cooking time:
about 35 minutes

Serves 4

Calories:
607 per portion

YOU WILL NEED:
575 g/1 ¼ lb canned tomatoes
olive oil
2 garlic cloves, each cut into 3-4 pieces
1 chilli
100 g/4 oz Calabrese salami, thickly
   sliced
salt
450 g/1 lb conchiglie
65 g/2 ½ oz pecorino cheese, grated

Prepare the sauce before cooking the pasta. Crush the tomatoes or blend them briefly in a liquidizer. Coat the bottom of a saucepan with olive oil. Add the garlic and chilli and fry gently until the garlic is golden, crushing the chilli against the bottom of the pan to release its flavour. Add the tomatoes and the slices of salami with salt to taste. Simmer gently for about 30 minutes, until the sauce becomes denser and darker in colour.

Meanwhile, cook the conchiglie in boiling, salted water until just tender (al dente). Drain, transfer to a serving dish and pour the sauce over the top. Serve with the grated pecorino.

■ COOK'S TIP

In Calabria this dish is served with grated ricotta which has been left to mature and is no longer a fresh curd cheese.

71   ROMAN GNOCCHI

Preparation time:
20-30 minutes, plus
firming

Cooking time:
30-40 minutes

Oven temperature:
220 C/425 F/gas 7

Serves 4-6

Calories:
434-289 per portion

YOU WILL NEED:
600 ml/1 pint milk
100 g/4 oz semolina
pinch nutmeg
salt and white pepper
100 g/4 oz Gruyère cheese, grated
25-50 g/1-2 oz butter, melted
25-50 g/1-2 oz Parmesan cheese, grated

Bring the milk to the boil. Remove from the heat and immediately add the semolina all at once. Beat well until smooth, season with a pinch of nutmeg and salt and pepper. Return to the heat, bring to the boil and cook for 5-7 minutes over a moderate heat, beating vigorously all the time until the mixture leaves the sides of the pan. Beat in the Gruyère cheese and check the seasoning.

Turn the mixture out on to a buttered or oiled baking tray and spread into a sheet approximately 1-1.5 cm/½-¾ inch thick. Leave until cold then refrigerate until completely firm.

Cut the gnocchi into rounds with a 5-6 cm/2-2½ inch pastry cutter and arrange the rounds, overlapping, in a buttered oven-proof dish. (Re-form leftover mixture and cut out more rounds.) Pour the melted butter over the top and sprinkle the Parmesan cheese over. Bake in a preheated oven for 20-30 minutes until golden brown. Serve at once.

72   TAGLIOLINI WITH SMOKED SALMON SAUCE

Preparation time:
10 minutes

Cooking time:
about 10 minutes

Serves 4

Calories:
537 per portion

YOU WILL NEED:
450 g/1 lb tagliolini
salt
50 g/2 oz smoked salmon
25 g/1 oz butter
200 ml/7 fl oz single cream
1 tablespoon grated Parmesan cheese

Cook the tagliolini in boiling salted water until just tender (al dente). Prepare the sauce while the pasta is cooking, or just before if fresh pasta is being used.

Cut the salmon into short, thin strips. Melt the butter in a large saucepan and add the cream. Heat through and add the smoked salmon and salt to taste. Stir in a ladle of the boiling pasta cooking water.

Drain the pasta, transfer it to a serving dish and pour the sauce over the top, adding the grated cheese and mixing thoroughly. Serve immediately as it is.

■ COOK'S TIP

To make this dish more substantial, cut 175 g/6 oz bacon rashers into strips. Fry them gently in a little oil and sprinkle over the gnocchi in the baking dish.

■ COOK'S TIP

Look out for salmon offcuts in delicatessens or buy frozen salmon offcuts in a supermarket. Cheese is not usually used in fish sauces, but this an exception.

73 SEDANI WITH SORRENTO SAUCE

Preparation time:	YOU WILL NEED:
15 minutes	575 g/1 ¼ lb canned tomatoes
	olive oil
Cooking time:	2 garlic cloves, each cut into 3-4 pieces
about 20 minutes	1 small chilli
	bunch of fresh basil, coarsely chopped
Serves 4	salt
Calories:	450 g/1 lb sedani
686 per portion	275 g/10 oz mozzarella cheese, cut into
	1 cm/ ½ inch cubes

Start making the sauce before cooking the pasta. Crush the tomatoes or blend them briefly in a liquidizer. Coat the bottom of a frying pan with olive oil. Add the garlic and chilli and fry gently until the garlic is golden, crushing the chilli against the bottom of the pan to release its flavour. Add the tomatoes and a third of the chopped basil with salt to taste and simmer gently for about 15 minutes, until the sauce becomes denser.

Meanwhile, cook the sedani in boiling, salted water until just tender (al dente). Drain, transfer to a serving dish and pour the sauce over the top. Mix the sauce with the sedani and the remaining chopped basil. Add the mozzarella cubes but do not stir. Serve individual portions with grated Parmesan.

74 RIGATONI WITH COURGETTE SAUCE

Preparation time:	YOU WILL NEED:
15 minutes	olive oil
	2 onions, finely chopped
Cooking time:	8 courgettes, thinly sliced
15-20 minutes	salt
Serves 4	450 g/1 lb rigatoni
	50 g/2 oz Parmesan cheese, grated
Calories:	
539 per portion	

Start making the sauce before cooking the rigatoni. Coat the base of a large frying pan with olive oil and fry the onions gently until transparent. Add the courgettes halfway through the onion cooking time and fry them gently until just tender. Stir frequently to prevent them sticking. Cover the pan if the courgettes tend to burn on the outside before being cooked through. Add salt to taste.

Meanwhile, cook the rigatoni in boiling, salted water until just tender (al dente). When draining the pasta, collect a small quantity of the cooking water in a bowl placed under the colander. Transfer the rigatoni to a serving dish and mix in the courgettes and onions, adding a ladle of the cooking water and the Parmesan to form a moist, creamy mixture. Serve immediately with a little extra Parmesan if liked.

■ COOK'S TIP

The mozzarella will begin to melt on contact with the hot pasta and sauce. Do not stir the cubes into the pasta as they will stick together to form a solid piece of cheese again. The chilli may be omitted and chilli oil served with individual portions.

■ COOK'S TIP

Should any courgette flowers still be attached, they can be washed, sliced and added to the courgettes and onions while frying. The flowers have a very delicate flavour.

75 CARAMELLI WITH BASIL SAUCE

Preparation time:
10 minutes

Cooking time:
about 10 minutes

Serves 4

Calories:
638 per portion

YOU WILL NEED:
350 g/12 oz wholemeal caramelli shells
salt and pepper
75 g/3 oz fresh basil leaves
4 tablespoons olive oil
3 garlic cloves, crushed
50 g/2 oz pine nuts, or blanched
　　slivered almonds
50 g/2 oz grated Parmesan cheese
25 g/1 oz softened butter

Cook the caramelli in boiling, salted water until just tender (al dente). Drain, refresh in hot water and drain again, tossing thoroughly to ensure that no water is trapped inside.

Meanwhile, make the sauce. Blend the herb leaves, oil, garlic and nuts in a liquidizer. Scrape out the mixture, beat in the cheese and butter and season with pepper.

Spoon the sauce over the caramelli and serve at once, as an accompaniment to meat and poultry, or on its own.

76 SPAGHETTI WITH OIL AND GARLIC SAUCE

Preparation time:
10 minutes

Cooking time:
5 minutes (for the sauce)

Serves 4

Calories:
911 per portion

YOU WILL NEED:
450 g/1 lb spaghetti
bunch of parsley
4 garlic cloves
200 ml/7 fl oz olive oil
1 ½ generous tablespoons pine nuts, or
　　roughly chopped almonds
1 generous tablespoon sultanas

Start making the sauce when you have dropped the pasta into boiling salted water to cook.

Wash, dry and roughly chop the parsley. Peel and cut each clove of garlic into three or four pieces.

Put the oil into a small saucepan and when it is hot, but not smoking, add the garlic and 'boil' until golden and crispy. Add the nuts, followed by the sultanas two minutes later. At this point add half the chopped parsley and a ladle of boiling pasta water, just before draining the pasta.

Divide the freshly cooked and drained pasta between four individual dishes, and pour the sauce over each one, taking care to divide the nuts and sultanas as evenly as possible.

Serve immediately, garnished with the remaining chopped parsley.

■ COOK'S TIP

If you do not have a plentiful supply of basil, experiment with other herbs. Both marjoram and mint make interesting – though entirely different – substitutes.

■ COOK'S TIP

The secret of this sauce is to get the timing right. It should be ready at the same time as the pasta. It takes quite a bit of practice to do it perfectly. Good luck!

77 CONCHIGLIE WITH CAULIFLOWER SAUCE

Preparation time:
10 minutes

Cooking time:
about 15 minutes

Serves 4

Calories:
493 per portion

YOU WILL NEED:
1 cauliflower, broken into florets
salt
10 black olives, stoned
1 tablespoon capers
olive oil
2 garlic cloves, cut into 3-4 pieces
450 g/1 lb conchiglie

Prepare the sauce before cooking the pasta. Boil the cauliflower in salted water until almost cooked. Strain, reserving about 150 ml/¼ pint of the cooking water. Cut each olive into three or four pieces. Rinse and dry the capers if they have been salted.

Coat the bottom of a large saucepan with olive oil and fry the garlic gently until golden. Add the capers and olives and fry gently for about 5 minutes, until they have begun to soften. Add the strained cauliflower and stir well, adding the reserved cooking water to keep the mixture moist.

Cook the conchiglie in boiling, salted water and drain it 2-3 minutes before it becomes tender. Add it to the cauliflower sauce in the pan and finish cooking the pasta in the cauliflower sauce, adding a little pasta cooking water if necessary to keep the mixture moist.

78 MACARONI WITH BROCCOLI

Preparation time:
15-20 minutes, plus soaking

Cooking time:
65 minutes

Serves 4

Calories:
635 per portion

YOU WILL NEED:
350 g/12 oz broccoli
salt and pepper
4 tablespoons olive oil
1 onion, sliced
450 g/1 lb tomatoes, skinned and mashed
1 garlic clove, crushed
6 canned anchovies, drained and soaked in milk
40 g/1 ½ oz seedless raisins, soaked in lukewarm water for 15 minutes
40 g/1 ½ oz pine nuts
350 g/12 oz macaroni
4 basil leaves, chopped
75 g/3 oz pecorino cheese, grated

Cook the broccoli in boiling salted water for 15 minutes. Drain thoroughly.

Heat half the oil in a heavy pan and fry the onion gently for 5 minutes. Add the tomatoes with salt and pepper to taste and simmer, covered, for 30 minutes. Heat the remaining oil in a separate pan and fry the garlic gently until browned. Add the anchovies and cook, stirring, until broken down. Add to the sauce with the raisins, broccoli and pine nuts. Cook for a further 5 minutes, stirring frequently.

Meanwhile, cook the macaroni in boiling, salted water until just tender (al dente). Drain thoroughly and pile into a warmed serving dish. Pour over the sauce, then fold in the basil and pecorino gently. Serve at once.

■ COOK'S TIP

Some people prefer to cook the pasta in the cauliflower water after the vegetable has been removed. Cheese is not usually served with this dish.

■ COOK'S TIP

Broccoli is often served cold in Italy with an oil and lemon juice dressing. Sicilians use the vegetable to make this unusual sauce.

79 FUSILLI WITH PEPERONI SAUCE

Preparation time:	YOU WILL NEED:
15 minutes	*2 red peppers, seeded*
	10 black olives, stoned
Cooking time:	*1 tablespoon capers*
about 15 minutes	*olive oil*
	salt
Serves 4	*450 g/1 lb fusilli*
	50 g/2 oz butter
Calories:	*100 g/4 oz Parmesan cheese, grated*
659 per portion	*milk*

Start making the sauce before cooking the fusilli. Cut the peppers into thin strips lengthways. Cut each olive into three or four pieces. Wash and dry the capers if they have been salted.

Coat the bottom of a large frying pan with olive oil and gently fry the peppers until tender, adding the olives and capers halfway through the cooking time. Add salt to taste. Strain off the excess olive oil.

Meanwhile, cook the fusilli in boiling, salted water until just tender (al dente). Drain, transfer it to a serving dish and pour the sauce over the top. Add the butter, Parmesan and a drop of milk and mix thoroughly. Add a little more milk if necessary to form a moist, creamy mixture.

Serve individual portions with extra Parmesan if liked.

80 SPAGHETTI WITH SARDINES

Preparation time:	YOU WILL NEED:
30-40 minutes	*1 head fennel, quartered*
	8-10 tablespoons olive oil
Cooking time:	*2 garlic cloves, crushed*
40-45 minutes	*450 g/1 lb sardines (see Cook's Tip)*
Oven temperature:	*2 large onions, thinly sliced*
200 C/400 F/gas 6	*1 tablespoon sultanas*
	1 tablespoon pine nuts
Serves 4	*6 anchovy fillets, chopped*
	2 tablespoons chopped parsley
Calories:	*150 ml/5 fl oz white wine or fish stock*
963 per portion	*salt and pepper*
	450 g/1 lb spaghetti
	lightly browned white breadcrumbs

Cook the fennel in boiling salted water until almost tender. Drain well, reserving the cooking liquid. Chop the fennel coarsely. Heat 3 tablespoons oil in a pan and add the garlic. Cook gently until golden brown, then add the sardines and cook gently for a further 10 minutes.

Meanwhile, heat another 3 tablespoons oil in a pan and cook the onions until they are soft and golden brown. Add the fennel, sultanas, pine nuts, anchovies, parsley, and wine. Season lightly. Cook over a moderate heat for 10 minutes.

Cook the spaghetti in boiling salted water to which the fennel water has been added. Drain well and place half in an oven-to-table dish. Cover with half the sardines and a little of the onions and fennel. Repeat the layers and sprinkle breadcrumbs and a little oil over the top. Cook in a preheated oven for 20 minutes.

■ COOK'S TIP

Fusilli is used with this sauce so that the long strips of pepper can wrap themselves around the twisted pasta. Peppers cooked in this way are served as a vegetable dish and consequently this sauce is often made with peppers left over from a previous meal.

■ COOK'S TIP

To prepare the sardines, bone them and remove the heads and tails. Cut each sardine into 2 or 3 pieces, depending on size, before cooking them.

81 FUSILLI WITH AUBERGINES AND TOMATO SAUCE

Preparation time:
20 minutes, plus draining

Cooking time:
40-45 minutes

Serves 4

Calories:
827 per portion

YOU WILL NEED:

1 large aubergine, diced

salt

120-150 ml/4-5 fl oz olive oil

450 g/1 lb fusilli

1 × quantity Tomato sauce (see Cook's Tip)

black pepper

1 tablespoon chopped fresh basil or parsley

Spread the diced aubergine on a wire cooking rack over a tray and sprinkle over 1-2 teaspoons salt. Leave for at least 30 minutes to drain. This will remove some of the liquid and strong flavour from the aubergines. Rinse thoroughly, drain well and dry on absorbent kitchen paper.

Heat half the oil in a frying pan and cook some of the aubergine dice until they are golden brown. Repeat, adding more oil to the pan if necessary until all the dice are cooked. Keep hot.

Cook the fusilli in boiling salted water for about 12 minutes until just tender (al dente). Drain well and stir into the hot tomato sauce. Check the seasoning and add salt and pepper to taste. Pour into a serving bowl and put the fried aubergine on top. Sprinkle the chopped basil or parsley over just before serving.

82 MUSHROOM RAVIOLI

Preparation time:
35-40 minutes

Cooking time:
40 minutes

Serves 4

Calories:
847 per portion

YOU WILL NEED:

2 tablespoons olive oil

1 medium onion, finely chopped

1-2 garlic cloves, crushed

450 g/1 lb mushrooms, finely chopped

200 g/7 oz ricotta cheese

1 egg, beaten

2-3 tablespoons white breadcrumbs

salt and pepper

1 × quantity Egg pasta dough (recipe 54)

75 g/3 oz butter

50 g/2 oz Parmesan cheese, grated

Heat the oil, add the onion and garlic, and cook gently until soft and lightly coloured. Add the mushrooms and continue to cook gently until the mushrooms are soft and any liquid has evaporated. Remove from the heat, beat in the ricotta and egg and sufficient breadcrumbs to give a firm mixture. Season.

Roll the pasta dough out thinly and cut out 6 cm/2½ inch rounds. Place a portion of the mixture on each, brush around the edge of the dough with cold water, fold over and seal.

Cook a few ravioli at a time for 4-5 minutes in boiling salted water. They are cooked when they rise to the surface. Remove with a draining spoon, drain well and place in a hot serving dish. Cover and keep hot until all the ravioli are cooked. Just before serving, heat the butter in a pan until it is a light golden brown and pour immediately over the ravioli. Sprinkle a little of the Parmesan cheese over and serve the rest separately. Serve hot.

■ COOK'S TIP

For Tomato sauce, gently fry 1 chopped onion, 2 crushed garlic cloves and 2 chopped rashers of streaky bacon in 1-2 tablespoons olive oil. When soft, add 1 × 400 g/14 oz can chopped tomatoes, seasoned. Simmer 25-30 minutes until thickened. For a smooth sauce, liquidize then sieve to remove seeds.

■ COOK'S TIP

Although most ravioli is cut into squares, when it is cooked in an Italian home or in a restaurant serving home cooking, it is often made half-moon shaped.

83 NOODLES WITH CHICKEN AND TOMATOES

Preparation time:
20 minutes

Cooking time:
15 minutes

Serves 4

Calories:
402 per portion

YOU WILL NEED:
1 tablespoon olive oil
100 g/4 oz boneless chicken breast,
  chopped
1 small onion, chopped
1 celery stick, chopped
1 carrot, chopped
1 teaspoon dried oregano
4 tablespoons red wine
1 × 225 g/8 oz can tomatoes
salt and pepper
350 g/12 oz fettuccine
celery leaves, to garnish

Heat the olive oil in a saucepan and fry the chicken until lightly coloured. Add the onion, celery and carrot and cook for 5 minutes or until softened. Add the oregano, wine, tomatoes, salt and pepper. Bring to the boil, reduce the heat, cover and cook for 10 minutes.

Meanwhile, cook the fettuccine in boiling, salted water until just tender (al dente). Drain thoroughly and mix with the chicken sauce. Transfer to a serving dish and garnish with celery leaves.

84 MUSHROOM LASAGNE

Preparation time:
25 minutes

Cooking time:
about 35 minutes

Oven temperature:
190 C/375 F/gas 5

Serves 4

Calories:
683 per portion

YOU WILL NEED:
2 tablespoons olive oil
1 large onion, chopped
225 g/8 oz button mushrooms, sliced
1 tablespoon plain flour
1 tablespoon lemon juice
600 ml/1 pint natural yogurt
salt and pepper
75 g/3 oz chopped walnuts
100 g/4 oz lean ham, in julienne strips
1 tablespoon chopped parsley
225 g/8 oz cooked wholemeal lasagne
175 g/6 oz Wensleydale cheese, grated
6 tablespoons wholemeal breadcrumbs

Heat the oil and fry the onion over moderate heat for 3 minutes, stirring frequently. Add the mushrooms and cook for 2 minutes. Stir in the flour and cook for 1 minute. Remove the pan from the heat and gradually stir in the lemon juice and half the yogurt. Cook, stirring, over low heat until the mixture thickens, then season. Simmer 2 minutes. Stir in the walnuts, ham and parsley and remove from the heat. Pour a layer of this mixture into a greased baking dish. Cover with sheets of cooked lasagne (see Cook's Tip) and continue making layers, finishing with a layer of lasagne.

Stir the remaining yogurt and half the cheese together and pour over the dish. Sprinkle over the remaining cheese mixed with the breadcrumbs. Put the dish on a baking tray and bake in a preheated oven for 25-30 minutes, or until golden brown.

■ COOK'S TIP

Dried herbs should be stored in airtight jars in a cool, dark place so that they do not lose their flavour or colour.

■ COOK'S TIP

Cook the lasagne sheets in plenty of boiling, salted water until just tender (al dente). Drain, rinse in cold water and drain again. Pat dry with absorbent paper.

85 SPAGHETTI WITH TOMATO AND BASIL SAUCE

Preparation time:
10 minutes

Cooking time:
about 35 minutes

Serves 4

Calories:
601 per portion

YOU WILL NEED:
7 tablespoons olive oil
1 onion, chopped
800 g/1 ¾ lb ripe tomatoes, chopped
1 tablespoon chopped basil
salt and pepper
400 g/14 oz spaghetti

Heat the oil in a heavy pan, add the onion and fry gently for 5 minutes. Add the tomatoes and basil with salt and pepper to taste. Cook gently for 30 minutes.

Meanwhile, cook the spaghetti in boiling, salted water until just tender (al dente). Drain thoroughly and pile into a warmed serving dish. Pour the sauce over the top and serve immediately.

86 BUCATINI WITH AMATRICE SAUCE

Preparation time:
15 minutes

Cooking time:
about 40 minutes

Serves 4

Calories:
639 per portion

YOU WILL NEED:
4 rashers rindless lean streaky bacon
2 × 400 g/14 oz cans tomatoes
olive oil
1 chilli
1 onion, finely chopped
1 tablespoon tomato purée
salt
450 g/1 lb bucatini
100 g/4 oz pecorino or romano cheese, grated

Start making the sauce before cooking the pasta. Cut the bacon into 1 cm/½ inch squares. Crush the tomatoes or blend them briefly in a liquidizer. Coat the bottom of a large frying pan with olive oil and add the chilli and onion. Fry the onion gently until transparent and crush the chilli against the bottom of the pan to release its flavour. Add the bacon and fry until crispy, stirring all the time. Add the tomato purée and the tomatoes with salt to taste and simmer gently for about 30 minutes, until the sauce becomes denser and darker in colour. Meanwhile, cook the bucatini in boiling, salted water until just tender (al dente) then drain, put half the cheese in a serving dish, add the freshly cooked pasta and pour the sauce over the pasta while mixing it with the remaining cheese. Serve individual portions with more grated cheese if desired.

■ COOK'S TIP

If the tomatoes do not have a sufficiently pronounced flavour, try adding a tablespoon of tomato purée to the sauce a few minutes before serving.

■ COOK'S TIP

The pasta called bucatini is a thick spaghetti with a hole through the centre. It originated in Rome where it is often served with the sauce named after Amatrice, a *small town to the north-east of the city.*

87 FUSILLI WITH BROCCOLI SPEARS

Preparation time:
20 minutes

Cooking time:
about 20 minutes

Serves 4

Calories:
608 per portion

YOU WILL NEED:
350 g/12 oz fusilli
salt and pepper
450 g/1 lb broccoli spears, blanched
(see Cook's Tip)
1 tablespoon olive oil
15 g/½ oz butter
1 small onion, finely chopped
40 g/1 ½ oz walnuts, roughly chopped
40 g/1 ½ oz anchovy fillets, chopped
1 tablespoon chopped parsley
25 g/1 oz grated Parmesan cheese

Cook the fusilli in boiling, salted water until just tender (al dente). Drain immediately, refresh in hot water, and then drain once more.

Meanwhile, heat the oil with the butter and fry the onion over low heat for 10 minutes, stirring occasionally. Stir in the walnuts, anchovies and broccoli and cook slowly over gentle heat for 3-4 minutes.

Stir in the pasta and heat through. Remove from the heat, add the parsley, season well with pepper and stir in the cheese. Serve at once.

88 LINGUINE WITH CREAM OF PRAWN SAUCE

Preparation time:
15 minutes

Cooking time:
about 10 minutes

Serves 4

Calories:
514 per portion

YOU WILL NEED:
450 g/1 lb linguine
salt
25 g/1 oz butter
200 ml/7 fl oz single cream
1 teaspoon tomato purée
150 g/5 oz peeled, cooked prawns,
roughly chopped
1 tablespoon chopped parsley, to
garnish

Cook the linguine in boiling, salted water until just tender (al dente). Meanwhile, make the sauce. Melt the butter in a large saucepan or deep frying pan, add the cream and the tomato purée and heat through. Add the prawns and salt to taste. Stir in a ladle of the pasta cooking water.

Drain the freshly cooked pasta, transfer it to a serving dish and pour the sauce over the top. Serve individual portions garnished with chopped parsley.

■ COOK'S TIP

Blanch the broccoli by cooking it in boiling, salted water for 5 minutes. Drain and plunge immediately into ice-cold water to prevent further cooking. Drain again.

■ COOK'S TIP

If liked, add a chilli while melting the butter and rub it against the bottom of the pan to release its flavour. Remove the chilli before serving the sauce.

89 BAKED MACARONI WITH PRAWNS

Preparation time:
15-20 minutes

Cooking time:
35-40 minutes

Oven temperature:
200 C/400 F/gas 6

Serves 4

Calories:
576 per portion

YOU WILL NEED:
90 g/3 ½ oz butter
175 g/6 oz button mushrooms, sliced
salt and pepper
225 g/8 oz peeled prawns
2 tablespoons brandy
50-75 g/2-3 oz Parmesan cheese, grated
225 g/8 oz short macaroni
300 ml/10 fl oz Béchamel sauce (recipe
    57 and Cook's Tip below)
pinch nutmeg

Heat half the butter in a pan and cook the mushrooms until tender. Season to taste with salt and pepper. Add the prawns and heat through then pour on the warmed brandy and set alight. When the flames have subsided, stir in half the cheese and check the seasoning.

Meanwhile, cook the pasta in boiling salted water until just tender (al dente). Drain well. Check the seasoning of the Béchamel sauce and add a pinch of nutmeg and the remainder of the cheese. Place a third of the macaroni in a buttered oven-to-table dish and spread half the mushroom mixture over. Repeat the layers, ending with a layer of macaroni. Cover with the Béchamel sauce. Heat the remaining butter in a pan and when it is lightly coloured pour it over the top. Bake in a preheated oven for about 20 minutes until golden brown. Serve hot.

90 POTATO GNOCCHI

Preparation time:
20-30 minutes

Cooking time:
30-40 minutes

Serves 4

Calories:
545 per portion

YOU WILL NEED:
750 g/1 ½ lb old floury potatoes, peeled
    and cut into even-sized pieces
175-200 g/6-7 oz plain flour
2 egg yolks, beaten
salt and white pepper
pinch nutmeg
50-75 g/2-3 oz melted butter
50 g/2 oz Parmesan cheese, grated

Cook the potatoes in boiling salted water until tender. Drain well and return to the heat for a few moments, shaking the pan all the time to dry out the potatoes. Sieve the potatoes through a vegetable mill or mash until quite smooth. Beat in most of the flour and the egg yolks and mix until smooth.

Turn out on to a floured board and knead in more flour, if necessary, to give a firm mixture. Roll the potato mixture out into sausage strips about 1 cm/½ inch in diameter and cut into 3 cm/1¼ inch pieces. Press the centre of each piece lightly between thumb and forefinger or with a fork to flatten them slightly.

Cook the gnocchi, a few at a time, in a large pan of gently boiling water. They are cooked when they rise to the surface. Remove with a draining spoon, and drain well. Place in a hot buttered dish and keep hot until all the gnocchi are cooked. Just before serving, pour the hot melted butter over the top. Sprinkle a little Parmesan cheese over and serve the rest separately.

■ COOK'S TIP

For a more economical dish use cod or smoked haddock which has been skinned, poached in water and broken into chunks with a fork. For 300 ml/10 fl oz Béchamel sauce, use 25 g/1 oz butter, 25 g/1 oz flour and 300 ml/10 fl oz milk. Make as in recipe 57.

■ COOK'S TIP

Make certain the potatoes don't overcook. Take care not to overload the pan of water with gnocchi: they need room to move in the water.

91 RIBBON NOODLES WITH PARMESAN AND BUTTER

Preparation time:
15 minutes

Cooking time:
about 10 minutes

Serves 4

Calories:
588 per portion

YOU WILL NEED:
400 g/14 oz fettuccine
salt and pepper
75 g/3 oz Parmesan cheese, grated
65 g/2 ½ oz butter, softened
pinch of grated nutmeg
1 white truffle or a few button mushrooms, thinly sliced

Cook the fettuccine in boiling, salted water until just tender (al dente). Drain thoroughly, then pile in a warmed serving dish. Add the Parmesan, butter and nutmeg with salt and pepper to taste and fold gently to mix. Top with the thinly sliced truffle or mushrooms and serve immediately with a well-flavoured meat ragú if liked.

92 SPAGHETTI WITH OLIVES

Preparation time:
15 minutes

Cooking time:
about 25 minutes

Serves 4

Calories:
810 per portion

YOU WILL NEED:
150 ml/ ¼ pint olive oil
1 yellow or green pepper, cored, seeded and sliced
3 tomatoes, skinned and chopped
salt and pepper
100 g/4 oz black olives, halved and stoned
400 g/14 oz spaghetti
65 g/2 ½ oz pecorino or Parmesan cheese, grated

Heat the oil in a heavy pan, add the yellow or green pepper and tomatoes with salt and pepper to taste. Cover and simmer gently for 20 minutes, stirring occasionally. Add the olives and cook for 5 minutes.

Meanwhile, cook the spaghetti in boiling, salted water until just tender (al dente). Drain thoroughly and add to the sauce. Fold gently to mix, then pile into a warmed serving dish and sprinkle with the cheese. Serve immediately.

■ COOK'S TIP

White truffles are in reality a brownish colour on the outside. They have a very powerful flavour and aroma, quite different from that of black truffles. The best and largest come from the country around Alba. Specially trained dogs search out these delicacies.

■ COOK'S TIP

If you have opened a can of olives, transfer unused ones to a screw-top jar. Place a slice of lemon over the olives in the jar to keep them fresh. Store in the refrigerator.

93 SPAGHETTI WITH EGG AND BACON

Preparation time: 15 minutes	YOU WILL NEED: 25 g/1 oz butter
	100 g/4 oz bacon, diced
Cooking time: 10-15 minutes	1 garlic clove
	400 g/14 oz spaghetti
Serves 4	salt and pepper
	3 eggs, beaten
Calories 633 per portion	40 g/1 ½ oz Parmesan cheese, grated
	40 g/1 ½ oz pecorino cheese, grated

Melt the butter in a heavy pan, add the bacon and garlic, fry gently until browned, then remove the garlic from the pan.

Cook the spaghetti in boiling, salted water until just tender (al dente). Drain thoroughly and add to the bacon. Stir well, then remove from the heat. Add the eggs, a pinch of pepper, half the Parmesan and half the pecorino. Toss until the eggs turn creamy yellow, then add the remaining cheeses. Toss again and serve immediately.

94 SPAGHETTI WITH CASSEROLE SAUCE

Preparation time: 10 minutes	YOU WILL NEED: 100 g/4 oz butter
	225 g/8 oz finely minced lean beef
Cooking time: about 15 minutes	225 g/8 oz button mushrooms, quartered
Serves 4	salt and pepper
	4 tablespoons dry white wine
Calories: 584 per portion	450 g/1 lb spaghetti
	100 g/4 oz Parmesan cheese, grated
	knob of butter

Start making the sauce before cooking the spaghetti. Melt the butter in an earthenware casserole and fry the minced beef gently, stirring thoroughly so that it does not stick together. Add the mushrooms and continue cooking until both the beef and mushrooms are cooked. Add salt to taste and a generous quantity of pepper. Pour in the wine and allow it to evaporate.

Meanwhile, cook the spaghetti in boiling water until just tender (al dente). Drain and mix thoroughly with the sauce, adding half the Parmesan and the butter. Serve individual portions immediately with the remaining Parmesan.

■ COOK'S TIP

Bacon dice tend to stick together so stir them frequently while they are frying. If the bacon is very fatty, reduce the amount of butter used for frying.

■ COOK'S TIP

A little of the pasta cooking water can be added when mixing everything together if the pasta looks like it may be too dry.

95 PAGLIA E FIENO WITH CIOCIARA-STYLE SAUCE

Preparation time:
10 minutes

Cooking time:
10-15 minutes

Serves 4

Calories:
818 per portion

YOU WILL NEED:
100 g/4 oz frozen peas
salt and pepper
225 g/8 oz button mushrooms, thinly sliced
50 g/2 oz butter or margarine
100 g/4 oz piece lean cooked ham
200 ml/7 fl oz single cream
450 g/1 lb paglia e fieno
100 g/4 oz Parmesan cheese, grated

Start making the sauce before cooking the pasta. Cook the peas in boiling, salted water and drain. Fry the mushroom gently in a knob of the butter or margarine until just tender, adding salt to taste. Trim any fat from the cooked ham and cut the ham into matchsticks.

Put the remaining butter into a saucepan with the cream and heat gently without allowing the mixture to boil. Add the mushrooms with their juice, the peas and the cooked ham.

Meanwhile, cook the paglia e fieno in boiling water until just tender (al dente). Add a ladle of the boiling pasta water and a third of the grated cheese to the sauce. Drain the pasta, transfer to a serving dish and pour the sauce over the top. Serve individual portions with grated Parmesan.

96 RIBBON NOODLES WITH HERBS AND BACON

Preparation time:
15 minutes

Cooking time:
about 15 minutes

Serves 4

Calories:
573 per portion

YOU WILL NEED:
3 tablespoons olive oil
100 g/4 oz fatty bacon or belly pork, chopped
1 onion, chopped
150 ml/¼ pint chicken stock
1 tablespoon chopped parsley
4 basil leaves, chopped
salt and pepper
400 g/14 oz fettuccine
65 g/2½ oz pecorino cheese, grated

Heat the oil in a heavy pan, add the bacon and onion and fry gently for 5 minutes. Add the stock, parsley, basil and salt and pepper to taste. Cook gently, stirring occasionally, until reduced and slightly thickened.

Meanwhile, cook the fettuccine in boiling, salted water until just tender (al dente). Drain thoroughly and pile into a warmed serving dish. Add the sauce and pecorino and fold gently to mix. Serve immediately.

■ COOK'S TIP

The Italian words paglia e fieno mean 'straw and hay'. These thin green and white ribbons of pasta are similar to fettuccine and are usually freshly made.

■ COOK'S TIP

A tomato salad makes a refreshing accompaniment to this dish of noodles. Slice the tomatoes thinly and spoon a little dressing on top about 20 minutes before serving.

97 MEZZE MANICHE WITH SPICY SAUSAGE SAUCE

Preparation time:
15 minutes

Cooking time:
about 45 minutes

Serves 4

Calories:
574 per portion

YOU WILL NEED:

575 g/1 ¼ lb canned tomatoes
1 onion, finely chopped
4 Italian-style spicy sausages
  olive oil
150 ml/¼ pint dry white wine
1 tablespoon concentrated tomato
  purée
salt
450 g/1 lb mezze maniche
50 g/2 oz Parmesan cheese, grated

Start making the sauce before cooking the pasta. Crush the tomatoes or blend them briefly in a liquidizer. Prick the sausages with a fork to prevent them from bursting and to allow the juices to flow into the sauce. Coat the bottom of a saucepan with olive oil. Fry the onion gently until transparent. Add the sausages and brown them lightly on all sides, then add the wine and allow it to evaporate. Add the tomato purée and tomatoes with salt to taste and simmer for about 40 minutes, until the sausages are thoroughly cooked and the sauce is denser. Remove the sausages and cut them into thinnish slices.

   Meanwhile, cook the mezze maniche in boiling, salted water until just tender (al dente). Drain, transfer to a serving dish and pour the sauce over the top, adding the sliced sausages and mixing well. Serve with grated Parmesan.

98 TRENETTE WITH PESTO GENOVESE

Preparation time:
20 minutes

Cooking time:
10-15 minutes

Serves 4

Calories:
803 per portion

YOU WILL NEED:

2 large bunches of basil
4 fresh mint leaves
1 garlic clove, roughly chopped
1 tablespoon pine nuts, or chopped
  almonds, or chopped walnuts
50 g/2 oz pecorino cheese, grated
about 150 ml/¼ pint olive oil
450 g/1 lb trenette

Start making the pesto just before cooking the pasta. Put the basil, mint and garlic on a large chopping board and chop them together finely until a very thick paste is formed, adding the nuts and part of the grated cheese as you chop. Scrape the mixture into a bowl, add the remaining grated cheese and gradually beat in the olive oil. Just before draining the trenette, take a ladle of boiling pasta water and mix it with the pesto in the bowl. Transfer the trenette to a serving dish, and pour the pasta over the top, adding a little more of the pasta water if necessary. The pesto should be thick and creamy and coat the trenette. Serve individual portions with a little extra pecorino or with Parmesan cheese if desired.

■ COOK'S TIP

This is a fairly substantial dish which can be served as a one-course meal, especially if a couple of extra sausages are added.

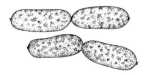

■ COOK'S TIP

The basil, mint, garlic and nuts can be put in a food processor and the cheese and oil added afterwards. This reduces the preparation time considerably and the results *are still excellent. Parmesan can be substituted for pecorino if preferred.*

99 GREEN NOODLES WITH BLUE CHEESE

Preparation time: 15 minutes	YOU WILL NEED: 350 g/12 oz green spinach noodles (see recipe 55)
Cooking time: 10 minutes	salt and pepper 6 rashers rindless streaky bacon, chopped
Serves 4	225 g/8 oz cottage cheese 50 g/2 oz Roquefort cheese, crumbled
Calories: 487 per portion	2 spring onions, thinly sliced

Cook the noodles in boiling, salted water until just tender (al dente). Drain, refresh in hot water, and drain again.

Meanwhile, fry the bacon over moderate heat until the fat has run and the bacon is crispy. Remove with a slotted spoon and reserve.

Toss the noodles with the cheeses and spring onions and season with salt and pepper. Stir in the chopped bacon. Transfer the noodles to a heated serving dish and serve at once.

100 MACARONI IN TOMATO SAUCE

Preparation time: 30-35 minutes, plus drying	YOU WILL NEED: 400 g/14 oz plain flour salt and pepper
Cooking time: about 35 minutes	4 eggs, beaten 1 tablespoon olive oil FOR THE SAUCE
Serves 4	7 tablespoons olive oil 2 garlic cloves, crushed
Calories: 687 per portion	800 g/1 ¾ lb tomatoes, skinned and mashed 1 tablespoon chopped parsley

To make the pasta, sift the flour and a pinch of salt on to a work surface, then make a well in the centre. Add the eggs and oil and mix together to a smooth dough. Roll the dough into a paper-thin sheet. Fold the dough over on itself several times, then cut it into fairly long slices. Cut these slices into strips about 6 cm/2½ inches long. Wind the strips tightly around a thick knitting needle to make small cylindrical shapes. Arrange the macaroni in a single layer on a cloth sprinkled with flour, then leave to dry for 1 hour.

To make the sauce, heat the oil in a heavy pan, add the garlic and fry gently for 5 minutes. Add the tomatoes with salt and pepper to taste. Bring to the boil, then simmer for 30 minutes. Meanwhile, cook the macaroni in boiling, salted water until just tender (al dente). Drain thoroughly and pile into a warmed serving dish. Pour over the sauce and sprinkle with the parsley.

▓ COOK'S TIP

This is a good way of using any leftover pieces of blue cheeses. The Italian blue cheese, gorgonzola, may be used instead of the Roquefort.

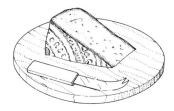

▓ COOK'S TIP

If you do not have time to make the macaroni, commercial dried pasta can be used instead for this recipe.

MEAT

Meat, especially pork and the very popular veal, plays a big part in the Italian diet. Beef, grown mostly on the rich pastures of the north, and lamb and kid are also popular, while offal is used a great deal. Recipes here come from all parts of Italy and use a good variety of other ingredients with the meat.

101 PORK WITH BAY LEAVES

Preparation time:
10 minutes

Cooking time:
1½-2 hours

Serves 4-6

Calories:
429-286 per portion

YOU WILL NEED:
2 tablespoons olive oil
1-1.25 kg/2-2 ½ lb boned loin of pork
    without rind, tied to a neat shape
1 tablespoon juniper berries, coarsely
    crushed
2 cloves
10 bay leaves, fresh if possible
2 large onions, chopped
salt and pepper
300 ml/10 fl oz dry white wine
150-450 ml/5-15 fl oz chicken stock

Heat the olive oil in a heavy-based pan or flameproof casserole just large enough to hold the meat. Brown the meat on all sides. Add the juniper berries, cloves, bay leaves, and onion and stir in to the oil. Season to taste with salt and pepper and pour on the white wine. Cover with a piece of greaseproof paper and a tight-fitting lid and cook very gently for 1½ hours or until tender. Avoid removing the lid too often but check once or twice while the meat is cooking, adding a little stock if necessary.

Remove the meat from the pan, slice and arrange on a serving dish. Cover and keep hot. Add sufficient stock to the pan to work all the browned residue into the stock. Bring to the boil, check the seasoning. Strain the liquid, if liked, and pour a little over the meat, serving the rest separately. Serve hot.

■ COOK'S TIP

You can, if you prefer, cook the meat in a preheated moderate oven (180 C/350 F/ gas 4). Do take care that the greaseproof paper does not hang over the sides of the pan by more than 1 cm/ ½ inch. Too much paper could be a fire hazard, especially on a gas flame.

102 OXTAIL STEW

Preparation time:
10 minutes, plus
soaking

Cooking time:
4½ hours

Serves 8

Calories:
366 per portion

YOU WILL NEED:
2 kg/4 ½ lb oxtail, cut into pieces
2 onions
2 carrots
575 g/1 ¼ lb celery
2 bay leaves
salt and pepper
1 tablespoon olive oil
225 g/8 oz lean bacon, chopped
50 g/2 oz raw ham, chopped
7 tablespoons dry white wine
450 g/1 lb tomatoes, skinned and
    mashed
pinch of ground cinnamon

Soak the oxtail in cold water for 2 hours. Put 1 onion, 1 carrot, 1 celery stick and the bay leaves in a large pan of salted water and bring to the boil. Add the oxtail pieces and bring to the boil. Boil for 1 hour, skimming frequently. Drain the oxtail, reserving the cooking liquid.

Chop the remaining onion and carrot. Heat the oil in a large clean pan, and add the onion, carrot, bacon, ham and oxtail. Fry, stirring, over moderate heat for 10 minutes, then add the wine and simmer until it has evaporated. Add the tomatoes, cover and simmer for 2½ hours, adding a little of the reserved cooking liquid from time to time as necessary.

Chop the remaining celery into 2 cm/¾ inch long pieces. Cook in boiling salted water for 10 minutes, then drain and add to the oxtail. Cook for a further 30 minutes, then add the cinnamon and a little pepper. Serve hot.

■ COOK'S TIP

Oxtail is usually sold already cut, sometimes with the pieces tied together in a neat round. If the tail is still in a piece, ask the butcher to cut it up for you.

103 MILANESE PORK STEW

Preparation time:
20-25 minutes

Cooking time:
2-2½ hours

Serves 4-6

Calories:
986-657 per portion

YOU WILL NEED:
275 g/10 oz pork rind
25 g/1 oz butter
3-4 tablespoons olive oil
2 large onions, sliced
2 large carrots, sliced
600 g/1¼ lb boneless pork, diced
150 ml/5 fl oz dry white wine
1.5 litres/2½ pints chicken stock
salt and pepper
225 g/8 oz Italian pork sausage or
    continental sausage cut into
    2.5 cm/1 inch slices
750 g/1½ lb Savoy cabbage, trimmed
    and shredded

Place the pork rind in a pan, cover with water and salt lightly. Bring to the boil and cook for 10 minutes. Drain and cut the rind into 5 cm × 1 cm/2 inch × ½ inch strips.

Heat the butter and half the oil in another pan. Cook the onion until soft but without colour, then add the carrots and celery and cook for about 5 minutes, stirring frequently.

Take the vegetables from the pan. Heat the remaining oil and cook the pork until it is well sealed. Return the vegetables and pork rind to the pan and pour on the white wine and the stock. Season to taste with salt and pepper. Simmer gently for 1½-2 hours until the meat is almost tender. Add the sausage and the cabbage and continue cooking for a further 25-30 minutes. Taste and adjust the seasoning and transfer to a serving dish. Serve hot.

■ COOK'S TIP

This dish is better made the day before it is required. Refrigerate it when cold and reheat the next day.

104 MEAT KEBABS WITH POLENTA

Preparation time:
25 minutes

Cooking time:
40-50 minutes

Oven temperature:
220 C/425 F/gas 7

Serves 4

Calories:
887 per portion

YOU WILL NEED:
1.5 litres/2½ pints water
400 g/14 oz maize flour
225 g/8 oz lean veal, cubed
225 g/8 oz lean pork, cubed
100 g/4 oz calf's liver, cubed
100 g/4 oz pig's liver, cubed
100 g/4 oz streaky bacon or belly pork,
    cubed
12-16 sage leaves
4 tablespoons olive oil
salt and pepper
7 tablespoons dry white wine
3-4 tablespoons beef stock

Salt the water and bring it to the boil. Stir in the maize flour and cook, stirring frequently over low heat for about 40 minutes, until the polenta is smooth and thickened.

Meanwhile thread the meat on to skewers, alternating the different kinds and interspersing them with sage leaves. Place the skewers in a single layer in the grill pan. Sprinkle with the oil and salt and pepper to taste.

Grill under a preheated hot grill for about 20 minutes, turning the skewers over from time to time. Then transfer them to a roasting tin into which they fit snugly. Add the wine and stock and roast in a preheated oven for 20 minutes.

Spread the polenta in a warmed serving dish, then top with the skewers of meat. Serve sprinkled with the meat juices.

■ COOK'S TIP

The meats should all be cut up into cubes of roughly the same size: cubes of about 2 cm/¾ inch will let the meats cook evenly.

105 TUSCAN BEEF STEW

Preparation time:
10 minutes

Cooking time:
2½ hours

Serves 4

Calories:
484 per portion

YOU WILL NEED:
3-4 tablespoons olive oil
2 garlic cloves, crushed
1 teaspoon chopped rosemary
750 g/1 ¾ lb stewing beef, cut into
   cubes
pinch of ground mixed spice
salt and pepper
7 tablespoons red wine
5 tablespoons tomato purée
rosemary sprigs, to garnish

Heat the oil in a flameproof casserole, add the garlic and rosemary and fry gently for 5 minutes until browned. Add the meat, spice and salt and pepper to taste and fry until the meat is browned on all sides.

Add the wine and simmer until reduced slightly. Stir in the tomato purée, dissolved in a little warm water. Simmer, stirring, for 3 minutes, then add enough water to cover the meat. Bring to the boil.

Cover the casserole, lower the heat and simmer for 2 hours or until the meat is tender, stirring occasionally and adding more water as necessary to cover the meat. Serve hot, garnished with rosemary.

106 VEAL ESCALOPES WITH HAM, CHEESE AND TOMATOES

Preparation time:
15 minutes

Cooking time:
about 30 minutes

Oven temperature:
190 C/375 F/gas 5

Serves 4

Calories:
592 per portion

YOU WILL NEED:
4 tablespoons olive oil
½ onion, chopped
225 g/8 oz tomatoes, skinned and
   mashed
salt and pepper
4 veal escalopes, each 100 g/4 oz
plain flour for coating
2 eggs, beaten
dried breadcrumbs for coating
75 g/3 oz butter
4 slices prosciutto or cooked ham
4 slices Gruyère cheese

Heat the oil in a heavy pan, add the onion and fry gently for 5 minutes. Add the tomatoes and salt and pepper to taste, then cook gently for 20 minutes, stirring occasionally.

Meanwhile, beat the veal slices slightly, then coat lightly with flour. Dip into the beaten egg, then coat with breadcrumbs.

Melt two thirds of the butter in a large frying pan, add the veal and brown quickly on both sides. Transfer to a buttered ovenproof dish. Cover each piece of veal with a slice of ham and a slice of cheese. Sprinkle with a little salt and pepper.

Bake in a preheated oven for 5-10 minutes or until the cheese has melted. Place the veal on a warmed serving platter, pour over the sauce and serve immediately.

■ COOK'S TIP

Do not let the casserole contents boil briskly. Long slow simmering ensures the beef is tender and has taken on a delicious flavour from the wine and rosemary.

■ COOK'S TIP

Gruyère – either Swiss or French – is the ideal cheese for this dish since it melts without drawing threads.

107 LAMB WITH FENNEL AND TOMATOES

Preparation time:
15 minutes

Cooking time:
about 1 hour 10 minutes

Serves 4

Calories:
478 per portion

YOU WILL NEED:
5 tablespoons olive oil
1 kg/2 lb boned leg of lamb, cut into serving pieces
1 onion, chopped
400 g/14 oz tomatoes, skinned and mashed
salt and pepper
750 g/1 ½ lb fennel, quartered

Heat the oil in a flameproof casserole, add the meat and fry over moderate heat until lightly browned on all sides. Stir in the onion and fry for a further 5 minutes, then add the tomatoes and salt and pepper to taste. Lower the heat, cover and simmer for 40 minutes, adding a little water if the casserole becomes too dry during cooking.

Cook the fennel in boiling salted water for 20 minutes. Drain and reserve 200 ml/⅓ pint of the cooking liquid.

Add the fennel and the reserved cooking liquid to the casserole and continue cooking for about 20 minutes until the meat is tender; the casserole should be fairly dry. Serve hot.

■ COOK'S TIP

Fennel is a native of southern Europe, much used in Italian cookery. Its aniseed-like flavour complements lamb very well.

108 VENETIAN MARINATED BEEF

Preparation time:
25-30 minutes, plus marinating

Cooking time:
2¼-2¾ hours

Serves 6-8

Calories:
942-706 per portion

YOU WILL NEED:
300 ml/10 fl oz red wine vinegar
1 garlic clove, chopped
2 cloves
pinch cinnamon
2 carrots, chopped
2 sticks celery, chopped
sprig each rosemary, thyme
salt and pepper
1 × 3.5 kg/3-3 ½ lb joint topside or top rump (see Cook's Tip)
75 g/3 oz butter
1 large onion, chopped
300 ml/10 fl oz dry white wine
300 ml/10 fl oz Marsala

Mix together the vinegar, garlic, cloves, cinnamon, carrots, celery, and herbs and season well. Place the meat in a deep dish and pour over the marinade. Cover and refrigerate for 12 hours, turning the meat frequently. Drain the meat and vegetables and dry them on absorbent kitchen paper. Discard the liquid. Heat the butter in a heavy-based pan and cook the onions, celery and carrots until soft. Remove the vegetables from the pan and add the meat. Brown well on all sides. Return the vegetables to the pan with the wine, Marsala and salt and pepper to taste. Cover the pan with a piece of greaseproof paper and a tight-fitting lid and cook over a gentle heat for 2-2½ hours until the meat is tender.

Cut the meat into thick slices and arrange on a hot dish. Check the seasoning and strain the sauce over the meat.

■ COOK'S TIP

To prepare the meat, remove all fat and retie it in a neat shape. This dish is traditionally eaten with polenta, a staple foodstuff of northern Italy (see recipe 104).

109 BEEF STEAKS PIZZAIOLO

Preparation time:
15-20 minutes

Cooking time:
25-35 minutes

Serves 4

Calories:
284 per portion

YOU WILL NEED:
75 ml/2 ½ fl oz olive oil
1-2 garlic cloves, crushed
450 g/1 lb tomatoes, peeled and
    chopped or 1 × 400 g/14 oz can
    chopped tomatoes
salt and pepper
1 teaspoon fresh chopped oregano or
    ½ teaspoon dried oregano
4 × 225 g/8 oz thinly cut beef steaks,
    trimmed of all fat

Heat three-quarters of the oil in a pan and cook the garlic gently until golden brown. Add the tomatoes, season lightly with salt and pepper and add the oregano. Bring to the boil and simmer for 10-15 minutes, until the sauce thickens slightly. Canned tomatoes will take longer than fresh ones.

Meanwhile heat the remaining oil in a frying pan and quickly brown the meat on both sides. Pour the sauce over and continue cooking very gently for 10-15 minutes, or until the meat is tender. If necessary, add a little water to prevent the sauce reducing too much.

Arrange the steaks on hot individual plates or a serving dish and pour the sauce over. Serve immediately.

110 LIVER TYROLESE-STYLE

Preparation time:
15 minutes, plus
soaking

Cooking time:
23-24 minutes

Serves 4

Calories:
602 per portion

YOU WILL NEED:
450 g/1 lb calf's liver, thinly sliced
250 ml/8 fl oz milk
50 g/2 oz butter
½ onion, chopped
50 g/2 oz streaky bacon, diced
25 g/1 oz plain flour
3 tablespoons stock
200 ml/⅓ pint double cream
1 tablespoon chopped capers
salt and pepper
sage leaves, to garnish

Put the liver and milk in a dish and leave for 1 hour.

Melt the butter in a frying pan, add the bacon and fry gently for 5 minutes. Drain the liver, then add to the pan and fry for 7-8 minutes.

Transfer the liver to a serving plate; keep hot. Mix the flour and stock to a smooth paste, then stir into the pan juices with the cream. Simmer for 10 minutes, stirring frequently. Add the capers and salt and pepper to taste. Pour over the liver and serve immediately, garnished with sage.

■ COOK'S TIP

This dish gets its name because it is cooked like a pizza with a topping of tomatoes, garlic and oregano. It is a very good recipe to use for steaks which are not *very tender or with pork chops. Simmer very gently until they tenderize, taking care that the sauce never boils as this would toughen the meat.*

■ COOK'S TIP

For a less expensive dish, use lamb's liver in place of the calf's liver. If the liver is frozen it will be easier to slice finely if the job is done before it has thawed fully.

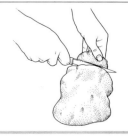

111 BEEF OLIVES

Preparation time:
20 minutes

Cooking time:
1 hour 15 minutes

Serves 4

Calories:
426 per portion

YOU WILL NEED:
2 young globe artichokes
juice of 1 lemon
8 slices beef topside, each 50 g/2 oz
100 g/4 oz prosciutto, finely chopped
50 g/2 oz butter
2 tablespoons olive oil
1 small onion, chopped
flour for coating
4-5 tablespoons dry white wine
salt and pepper
6-8 tablespoons hot beef stock

Discard the outer leaves, tips and chokes from the artichokes. Cook them in boiling salted water, with the lemon juice added, for 20 minutes. Drain and cut into 8 sections each.

Flatten the meat slices with a mallet. Mix the ham with a third of the butter and spread over the slices. Top each one with 2 artichoke sections, then roll the slices around the stuffing and tie securely with string.

Heat the remaining butter and the oil in a flameproof casserole, add the onion and fry gently for 5 minutes. Coat the meat rolls with flour, add to the casserole and fry, turning, until browned on all sides. Add the wine and salt and pepper to taste. Cover the casserole and cook gently for 45 minutes or until the meat is tender. Add stock as necessary to prevent the meat sticking.

Remove the meat from the casserole and untie the string. Arrange on a dish, then pour over the cooking juices.

112 STUFFED VEAL ROLLS

Preparation time:
15 minutes

Cooking time:
1 hour 10 minutes

Serves 4

Calories:
444 per portion

YOU WILL NEED:
4 tablespoons olive oil
225 g/8 oz mushrooms, chopped
1 garlic clove, crushed
1 tablespoon chopped parsley
4-6 tablespoons beef stock
salt and pepper
225 g/8 oz cooked pork, minced
75 g/3 oz Parmesan cheese, grated
1 egg, beaten
1 piece canned red pimento, chopped
8 veal escalopes, each 50 g/2 oz
350 g/12 oz tomatoes, skinned and
    mashed

Heat half the oil in a flameproof casserole, add the mushrooms, garlic and parsley and cook gently 15 minutes, adding stock to moisten if necessary. Season and transfer to a bowl. Add the pork, Parmesan, egg, and pimento; stir well to mix.

Beat the veal to flatten, season lightly and spread with the stuffing. Roll the veal up and tie securely.

Heat the remaining oil in the casserole, add the veal rolls and brown on all sides. Add the tomatoes with salt and pepper to taste, then cover and cook gently for about 45 minutes until the meat is tender. Turn the meat during cooking and add a few tablespoons of stock to moisten if necessary.

Take the meat from the casserole and untie the string. Arrange in a serving dish and pour over the cooking juices.

■ COOK'S TIP

Prosciutto is among the finest of Italian smoked hams. Only the best quality hams are used, and the salting process is long – hence the relatively high
price of a good prosciutto. If prosciutto is not available, use raw smoked ham in this recipe instead.

■ COOK'S TIP

Use a wooden mallet or a rolling pin with handles to beat the escalopes. The purpose is to stretch and flatten the meat, not beat it into holes.

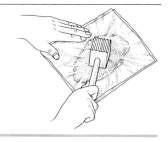

113 FILLET STEAK WITH HAM AND MUSHROOMS

Preparation time:
15 minutes

Cooking time:
26 minutes

Oven temperature:
180 C/350 F/gas 4

Serves 4

Calories:
358 per portion

YOU WILL NEED:
3 tablespoons olive oil
100 g/4 oz prosciutto or raw smoked
  ham, chopped
225 g/8 oz mushrooms, sliced
salt and pepper
1 tablespoon chopped parsley
8 slices beef fillet, each 50 g/2 oz
juice of ½ lemon

Heat half the oil in a flameproof casserole, add the ham, mushrooms and salt and pepper to taste and sauté for 5 minutes. Sprinkle with the parsley.

Arrange the beef slices on top, without overlapping the slices. Sprinkle with a little salt, the lemon juice and the remaining oil. Cook in a preheated oven for 20 minutes, turning the steaks and basting them with the cooking juices halfway through cooking. Serve immediately.

114 ROAST LAMB

Preparation time:
10 minutes

Cooking time:
1½ hours

Oven temperature:
190 C/375 F/gas 5

Serves 4

Calories:
467 per portion

YOU WILL NEED:
1 kg/2 lb leg of lamb
100 g/4 oz lean bacon, chopped
3 garlic cloves, slivered
2 rosemary sprigs
4 tablespoons olive oil
salt and pepper

Make deep incisions in the meat and insert the bacon, garlic and rosemary leaves. Use half of the oil to grease a roasting pan and put the lamb into the pan.

Sprinkle with salt and pepper and the remaining oil. Roast in a preheated oven for 1½ hours or until the meat is tender, basting occasionally. Transfer to a warmed serving dish and serve immediately.

■ COOK'S TIP

Tuscan beef is among the finest in the world. This recipe is a change from the usual cooking method, charcoal-grilling, and is ideal for small pieces of meat.

■ COOK'S TIP

Italians use rosemary a great deal to enhance the flavour of lamb. Sprigs of fresh rosemary are better than the dried herb for this dish.

115 LEG OF LAMB WITH TOMATOES

Preparation time:
20 minutes

Cooking time:
1 hour, 5 minutes

Oven temperature:
190 C/375 F/gas 5

Serves 4

Calories:
577 per portion

YOU WILL NEED:
50 g/2 oz lard
1 kg/2 lb boned leg of lamb, cut into
serving pieces
pinch of dried marjoram
400 g/14 oz potatoes, peeled and diced
225 g/8 oz pickling onions, peeled
225 g/8 oz tomatoes, skinned and
chopped
50 g/2 oz pecorino cheese, grated
750 ml/1 ¼ pints chicken stock
salt and pepper

Heat the lard in a flameproof casserole. Add the meat and fry, turning, until evenly browned. Add remaining ingredients, with salt and pepper to taste. Cover and cook in a preheated oven for 1 hour or until the meat is tender, stirring occasionally during cooking. Serve hot.

116 PORK CHOPS WITH SAGE AND ROSEMARY

Preparation time:
5 minutes

Cooking time:
approx 30 minutes

Oven temperature:
200 C/400 F/gas 6

Serves 4

Calories:
177 per portion

YOU WILL NEED:
4 pork chops, trimmed
salt and pepper
1 garlic clove, chopped
1 rosemary sprig, chopped
few sage leaves, chopped
7 tablespoons dry white wine

Sprinkle the chops with salt and pepper and place in an oiled baking tin. Sprinkle with the garlic, rosemary and sage, then add the wine and enough water to just cover the chops.

Bake in a preheated oven for about 30 minutes until tender. Transfer the chops to a warmed serving dish, pour over the cooking juices and serve immediately.

■ COOK'S TIP

Pecorino is a hard country cheese, excellent for grating and cooking. Look for straw-coloured cheese with a compact texture and a black or reddish-brown rind.

■ COOK'S TIP

For a healthy, low-fat dish carefully trim off the skin and fat from the edges of the chops before cooking them.

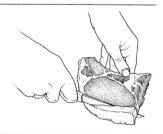

117 PORK SAUSAGES WITH BROCCOLI

Preparation time:
5 minutes

Cooking time:
about 50 minutes

Oven temperature:
190 C/375 F/gas 5

Serves 4

Calories:
526 per portion

YOU WILL NEED:
2-3 tablespoons vegetable oil
2 garlic cloves, crushed
1 piece of canned pimento
450 g/1 lb salamelle
salt and pepper
750 g/1 ½ lb broccoli

Heat the vegetable oil in a flameproof casserole, add the garlic and fry gently until browned. Stir in the pimento, sausages and salt and pepper to taste. Cover the casserole and bake in a preheated oven for about 45 minutes until the sausages are cooked.

Meanwhile, cook the broccoli in boiling salted water for 15 minutes until tender. Drain and place in a warmed serving dish. Add the sausages, toss well and serve immediately.

118 LAMB WITH FENNEL AND SWEET PEPPER

Preparation time:
15 minutes

Cooking time:
1 hour

Serves 4

Calories:
503 per portion

YOU WILL NEED:
1 × 1 kg/2 lb boned leg or shoulder of
    lamb
4 tablespoons olive oil, for frying
1 large onion, sliced
2 garlic cloves, crushed
1 × 400 g/14 oz can tomatoes
300 ml/½ pint beef stock
salt and pepper
2 fennel bulbs
2 red or yellow peppers, quartered,
    corded and seeded

Cut the meat into 4 cm/1½ inch cubes. Heat the oil in a flameproof casserole, add the meat and fry for about 5 minutes, until evenly browned. Add the onion and garlic and fry for a further 5 minutes.

Add the tomatoes, stock, salt and pepper and bring to the boil. Cover and simmer for 10 minutes.

Roughly chop the fennel leaves and reserve for garnish. Thickly slice the fennel bulbs. Add the peppers with the fennel bulbs to the pan. Cook for a further 30-35 minutes until the lamb is tender. Garnish with the chopped fennel leaves.

■ COOK'S TIP

Salamelle, or Salsiccia a metro, are long, thin, spiced sausages sold by the kilo in Italian delicatessens. Salamelle are often sold tied in short links and are available in several varieties, some peppery hot.

■ COOK'S TIP

This dish may be prepared up to 24 hours in advance and stored in the refrigerator. Store the garnish separately, in a plastic bag to prevent its scent penetrating other foods.

119 LAMB AND MUSHROOMS CASSEROLED IN WINE

Preparation time:
10 minutes

Cooking time:
1 hour 5 minutes

Oven temperature:
190 C/375 F/gas 6

Serves 4

Calories:
391 per portion

YOU WILL NEED:
3 tablespoons olive oil
1 kg/2 lb boned shoulder or leg of
*   lamb, cut into serving pieces*
450 g/1 lb mushrooms
4 fl oz/120 ml dry white wine
salt and pepper
chopped parsley, to garnish

Heat the oil in a flameproof casserole, add the meat and fry over moderate heat until browned on all sides. Add the mushrooms, wine and enough water to just cover the meat. Season with salt and pepper to taste.

Cover and cook in a preheated oven for 1 hour or until the meat is tender, stirring occasionally. Serve hot, garnished with the chopped parsley.

120 MARINATED POT ROASTED LAMB

Preparation time:
25 minutes, plus
marinating

Cooking time:
1¾ hours

Serves 4

Calories:
300 per portion

YOU WILL NEED:
Half a small leg or shoulder of lamb,
*   about 750 g/1 ½ lb*
1 stick celery, chopped
1 carrot, chopped
1 onion, chopped
6 juniper berries, bruised
300 ml/ ½ pint red wine
3 sprigs rosemary
2 garlic cloves, peeled
1 tablespoon olive oil, for frying
salt and pepper
1 tablespoon redcurrant jelly

Marinate the lamb in a large bowl with the celery, carrot, onion, juniper berries, wine, rosemary and garlic for up to 24 hours, turning occasionally. Remove the lamb and pat dry with absorbent kitchen paper.

Heat the oil in a flameproof casserole. Add the lamb and fry for about 5 minutes, until evenly browned. Add the marinade and salt and pepper to taste. Simmer very gently, covered, for 1½ hours until the lamb is very tender. Remove the meat and place in a warmed serving dish. Keep warm.

Strain the liquid through a sieve, pressing as much of the vegetable mixture through as possible. Return the liquid to the pan and add the redcurrant jelly. Bring to the boil and stir until the jelly has dissolved. Serve this sauce separately.

■ COOK'S TIP

Look out for ready-cut lamb pieces in the supermarket; preparation time will be reduced, since all you may need to do is trim fat from the meat.

■ COOK'S TIP

To carve either joint use a large sharp knife and a two-pronged fork with a thumb guard. Lamb is carved fairly thickly, starting near the largest bone.

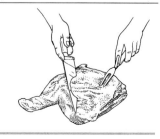

121 BEEF RISSOLES

Preparation time:
20 minutes

Cooking time:
10-15 minutes

Serves 4

Calories:
404 per portion

YOU WILL NEED:
350 g/12 oz cooked minced beef
2 garlic cloves, crushed
2 potatoes, boiled and mashed
1 tablespoon chopped parsley
75 g/3 oz Parmesan cheese, grated
1 stale bread roll, soaked in milk and
    squeezed dry
salt and pepper
1-2 eggs, beaten
dried breadcrumbs for coating
vegetable oil for shallow frying
parsley sprigs, to garnish

Put the beef in a bowl with the garlic, potato, parsley, Parmesan, bread and salt and pepper to taste. Add enough beaten egg to bind the mixture and stir until the ingredients are thoroughly combined. Shape the mixture into four oval rissoles, then coat in breadcrumbs.

Heat the oil in a frying pan. Add the rissoles and fry over moderate heat until golden brown on all sides. Drain on absorbent kitchen paper. Serve hot, garnished with parsley.

122 SWEET AND SOUR VEAL SWEETBREADS

Preparation time:
15-20 minutes

Cooking time:
25-30 minutes

Serves 4

Calories:
252 per portion

YOU WILL NEED:
25 g/1 oz butter
1 onion, chopped
½ carrot, chopped
1 small celery stick, chopped
25 g/1 oz streaky bacon, chopped
pinch of dried thyme
½ bay leaf, crumbled
450 g/1 lb calf's sweetbreads, cleaned
    and sliced
salt and pepper
3-4 tablespoons vinegar
25 g/1 oz sugar
3-4 tablespoons olive oil
25 g/1 oz capers

Melt the butter in a flameproof casserole, add the onion, carrot, celery, bacon, thyme and bay leaf and cook gently for 10 minutes. Add the sweetbreads and salt and pepper to taste. Cook gently for 15-20 minutes.

Meanwhile, heat the remaining ingredients in a small pan and cook gently, without boiling, for 5 minutes, stirring frequently with a wooden spoon. Put the sweetbread mixture in a warmed serving dish, pour over the sauce and serve immediately.

▇ COOK'S TIP

Use freshly grated Parmesan cheese, rather than the cheese sold ready-grated in tubs. The flavour will be much better.

▇ COOK'S TIP

Capers are the pickled flower buds of a shrub native to the Mediterranean, used in sauces, fish dishes and garnishes. They give a tangy flavour to this mild dish.

123 VEAL LIVER, PEASANT-STYLE

Preparation time:
10 minutes

Cooking time:
18-20 minutes

Serves 4

Calories:
368 per portion

YOU WILL NEED:
50 g/2 oz butter
50 g/2 oz streaky bacon, chopped
2 garlic cloves, chopped
1 tablespoon chopped parsley
2 onions, sliced
*450 g/1 lb calf's liver, cut into serving
  pieces*
25 g/1 oz plain flour
7 tablespoons red wine
freshly ground black pepper
salt

Melt the butter in a frying pan, add the bacon, garlic and half the parsley. Fry gently for 5 minutes. Add the onions and cook gently for 5 minutes, stirring frequently.

Coat the liver with the flour, add to the pan and brown lightly on both sides. Add the wine and a pinch of pepper. Cook for 5-6 minutes, stirring occasionally.

Add salt to taste and serve immediately, garnished with the remaining parsley.

124 VEAL AND HAM SLICES IN WINE

Preparation time:
10 minutes

Cooking time:
14-16 minutes

Serves 4

Calories:
403 per portion

YOU WILL NEED:
8 slices raw ham or bacon
8 veal escalopes, each 75 g/3 oz
8-12 sage leaves
50 g/2 oz butter
7 tablespoons dry white wine
salt and pepper
sage leaves, to garnish

Place a slice of ham on each slice of veal, then top with the sage leaves. Secure with cocktail sticks.

Melt the butter in a large frying pan, add the veal and fry until browned on both sides. Add the wine and salt and pepper to taste. Simmer for 6-8 minutes until the meat is tender.

Transfer the saltimbocca to a warmed serving platter, remove the cocktail sticks. Add 1 tablespoon water to the pan and simmer, stirring, for 1 minute then pour the pan juices over the saltimbocca. Garnish with sage and serve immediately.

■ COOK'S TIP

*Calf's liver is considered a
great delicacy in Italy, and
great care is taken in its
cooking to preserve its
tenderness and flavour.*

■ COOK'S TIP

*This classic Italian dish, from
the Lazio region, usually
figures on restaurant menus
as 'Saltimbocca alla
Romana'.*

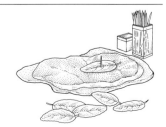

125 STUFFED BREAST OF LAMB

Preparation time:
15 minutes, plus
standing

Cooking time:
1 hour 40 minutes

Serves 4

Calories:
631 per portion

YOU WILL NEED:
100 g/4 oz salami, diced
100 g/4 oz provolone cheese, diced
25 g/1 oz Parmesan cheese, grated
25 g/1 oz fresh breadcrumbs
25 g/1 oz parsley, chopped
salt and pepper
1-2 eggs, beaten
1 kg/2 lb piece boned breast or
* shoulder of lamb*
3-4 tablespoons olive oil
1 onion, chopped
1 carrot, chopped
1 celery stick, chopped
1 garlic clove, crushed
150 ml/¼ pint dry white wine

Put the salami in a bowl with the cheeses, breadcrumbs, parsley and salt and pepper to taste. Stir well and mix in enough beaten egg to bind. Let stand 20 minutes.

Spread the mixture over the lamb and roll up the meat, tying securely with string. Heat the oil in a flameproof casserole, add the onion, carrot, celery and garlic, then place the meat on top. Season, then fry over moderate heat, turning the meat to brown. Add the wine and 2 tablespoons water, cover and cook gently for 1½ hours until the meat is tender, adding water to moisten as necessary.

Remove the meat from the casserole, untie and cut into neat slices. Arrange the slices on a warmed serving platter. Strain the cooking juices and pour over the meat.

126 MILANESE FRIED VEAL LIVER

Preparation time:
15 minutes, plus
marinating

Cooking time:
5-6 minutes

Serves 4

Calories:
467 per portion

YOU WILL NEED:
450 g/1 lb calf's liver, sliced
1 tablespoon chopped parsley
salt and pepper
4 tablespoons olive oil
plain flour for coating
2 eggs, beaten with a pinch of salt
dried breadcrumbs for coating
75 g/3 oz butter
FOR THE GARNISH
lemon slices
parsley sprigs

Place the liver in a shallow dish and sprinkle with the parsley, salt and pepper to taste and 2 tablespoons oil. Leave to marinate for 2 hours, turning occasionally.

Drain the liver, then coat lightly with flour. Dip in the beaten eggs, then coat with breadcrumbs.

Heat the remaining oil and the butter in a frying pan. Add the liver and fry over high heat for 4-5 minutes on each side until tender. Drain and serve immediately, garnished with lemon slices and parsley.

■ COOK'S TIP

In Italian cooking, provolone dolce, a young, mild cheese, is generally preferred to provolone piccante, which is a mature, more strongly flavoured cheese.

■ COOK'S TIP

This simple but sophisticated recipe for veal liver comes from the Lombardy region of Italy, famous for its many culinary specialities.

127 LAMB WITH CELERY AND ONIONS

Preparation time:
10 minutes

Cooking time:
approx 1 hour 10 minutes

Serves 4

Calories:
397 per portion

YOU WILL NEED:
3 tablespoons olive oil
2 celery sticks, chopped
350 g/12 oz pickling onions, peeled
1 kg/2 lb boned leg or shoulder of lamb, cut into serving pieces
2-3 rosemary sprigs, cut into pieces
2 bay leaves
salt and pepper
450 ml/¾ pint chicken stock

Heat the oil in a flameproof casserole, add the celery and onions and fry gently for 5 minutes. Add the meat, half the rosemary, the bay leaves and salt and pepper to taste. Fry over moderate heat until the meat is browned on all sides. Stir in the stock and enough water to just cover the meat. Cover the casserole and simmer for 1 hour or until the meat is tender. Discard the herbs.

Serve hot, garnished with the remaining rosemary.

128 VEAL AND APPLE RISSOLES

Preparation time:
15 minutes

Cooking time:
20 minutes

Serves 4

Calories:
356 per portion

YOU WILL NEED:
2 sharp eating apples, peeled, cored and finely chopped
450 g/1 lb minced veal
1 egg, beaten
1 ½ teaspoons sugar
salt and pepper
50 g/2 oz plain flour
65 g/2 ½ oz butter
4 tablespoons red wine

Put the apples in a bowl and add the meat, egg, sugar and salt and pepper to taste. Stir well to mix, adding a little of the flour to bind the mixture. Shape the mixture into rissoles and coat with flour.

Melt the butter in a large frying pan, add the rissoles and fry over moderate heat until browned on all sides. Add the wine, cover and cook gently for a further 15 minutes. Serve the rissoles hot.

■ COOK'S TIP

Shoulder of lamb has a higher fat content than leg, and it is a good idea to trim off all visible fat before cooking it.

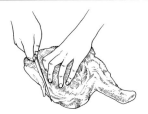

■ COOK'S TIP

This quickly prepared and cooked dish does not require top-quality expensive veal. Cut-up pieces of veal, often sold as 'pie veal', would be ideal for it.

129 LAMB IN EGG AND LEMON SAUCE

Preparation time:
15 minutes

Cooking time:
1 hour 20 minutes

Serves 6

Calories:
344 per portion

YOU WILL NEED:
50 g/2 oz lard
½ onion, finely chopped
50 g/2 oz raw ham or bacon, chopped
1 kg/2 lb boned shoulder of lamb, cut into cubes
pinch of grated nutmeg
salt and pepper
4 tablespoons dry white wine
450 ml/¾ pint chicken stock
2 eggs yolks
juice of ½ lemon
25 g/1 oz Parmesan cheese, grated
1 garlic clove, crushed
1 tablespoon chopped parsley

Melt the lard in a flameproof casserole, add the onion and ham and fry gently for 5 minutes. Add the lamb, nutmeg and salt and pepper to taste. Fry over moderate heat, turning the meat until it is browned on all sides. Add the wine and simmer until almost completely evaporated. Stir in the stock, cover and simmer for 1 hour or until the meat is tender.

Put the egg yolks in a bowl with the lemon juice and Parmesan cheese. Beat well to mix, then stir in a little of the hot cooking liquid. Add the garlic and parsley to the casserole, then gradually stir in the egg yolk mixture. Cook very gently, stirring constantly, until the sauce thickens; do not allow to boil or the sauce will curdle. Serve immediately.

130 VEAL ROLL WITH SPINACH

Preparation time:
15 minutes

Cooking time:
1¾ hours

Serves 4

Calories:
741 per portion

YOU WILL NEED:
2 eggs
75 g/3 oz Parmesan cheese, grated
salt and pepper
100 g/4 oz butter
450 g/1 lb cooked spinach, well drained and chopped
100 g/4 oz bacon rashers, derinded
1 × 800 g/1¾ lb slice leg of veal
3 tablespoons olive oil
120 ml/4 fl oz beef stock

Break the eggs into a bowl with a third of the Parmesan and a pinch each of salt and pepper. Beat well to mix. Melt 1 tablespoon of the butter in a frying pan, add the egg mixture and fry on both sides to make an omelet. Set aside.

Melt 1½ tablespoons butter in a heavy pan, add the remaining Parmesan and the spinach and cook, stirring, for a few minutes. Season, remove from the heat and leave to cool.

Spread the bacon over the veal, cover with the omelet, then top with the spinach. Roll the veal around the stuffing, then sew or tie securely.

Heat the oil and the remaining butter in a flameproof casserole, add the veal roll and fry, turning until browned on all sides. Sprinkle with salt and pepper to taste and add the stock. Cover and simmer for 1½ hours or until the meat is tender, basting occasionally with the pan juices. Remove the thread or tie and cut the veal into fairly thick slices. Serve hot.

■ COOK'S TIP

To reduce the calories in this dish replace the lard with 3-4 tablespoons vegetable oil and trim the visible fat off the meat well.

■ COOK'S TIP

Frozen wholeleaf spinach makes an acceptable substitute for fresh, if the latter is not available. Cook it from frozen and drain well before chopping it.

131 MILANESE VEAL ESCALOPES

Preparation time:
10 minutes

Cooking time:
5-7 minutes

Serves 4

Calories:
351 per portion

YOU WILL NEED:
4 veal escalopes, each 100 g/4 oz
1-2 eggs, beaten
dried breadcrumbs for coating
75 g/3 oz butter
salt and pepper
FOR THE GARNISH
lemon twists
parsley sprigs

Beat the veal lightly with a mallet to flatten. Dip into the beaten egg and coat with breadcrumbs.

Melt the butter in a large frying pan and fry the veal for 2-3 minutes on each side until tender and golden brown. Transfer to a warmed serving dish and sprinkle with salt and pepper to taste. Garnish with lemon and parsley and serve immediately.

132 VITELLO TONNATO

Preparation time:
30 minutes, plus
cooling

Cooking time:
1 hour

Serves 4

Calories:
729 per portion

YOU WILL NEED:
1 kg/2 lb boned leg of veal
1 large onion, quartered
2 cloves
bay leaf
2 sticks celery, chopped
2 carrots, chopped
8 peppercorns
1 × 200 g/7 oz can tuna fish, drained
2 egg yolks
4 anchovy fillets, finely chopped
2 tablespoons lemon juice
2 tablespoons capers
salt and pepper
175 ml/6 fl oz olive oil

Tie the veal into a neat shape. Place in a saucepan with the onion, cloves, bay leaf, celery, carrot and peppercorns and water to cover. Bring to the boil and skim off any scum. Reduce the heat, cover and simmer for 1 hour. Let the meat cool in the stock then remove.

Mash the tuna finely with a fork. Blend the egg yolks, anchovies, lemon juice, capers and a little salt and pepper in a liquidizer. While the machine is running pour in the olive oil in a fine steady stream until all the oil is added and the mayonnaise is thick and creamy. Add the tuna and blend until smooth. If the mayonnaise seems too thick add a spoonful of stock.

Cut the cold veal into thin slices and arrange in a serving dish. Spread the sauce over to enclose the meat completely. Cover the dish with foil and refrigerate at least 8 hours.

■ COOK'S TIP

Young, best-quality veal is essential for this recipe. Its fine texture ensures it cooks very quickly. It should not be overcooked.

■ COOK'S TIP

The traditional garnish for this classic dish is a lattice of anchovy fillets over the mayonnaise, with capers in between the lattice, and slices of lemon.

POULTRY &GAME

Poultry and game are widely available throughout Italy, and Italian cooks use them, both whole and in portions, in many excellent and unusual ways. Recipes here include imaginative dishes with chicken, turkey, small birds such as quail and partridge, and game, including rabbit, hare and venison.

133 CHICKEN IN GRAPE JUICE

Preparation time:
20-25 minutes

Cooking time:
50-55 minutes

Serves 4

Calories:
786 per portion

YOU WILL NEED:
3 tablespoons olive oil
4 × chicken quarters or breasts
1 medium onion, finely chopped
2 garlic cloves, crushed
2 tablespoons chopped parsley
450 g/1 lb white seedless grapes, stalks removed
salt and white pepper
3 tablespoons brandy
100 g/4 oz extra white seedless grapes
extra chopped parsley, to garnish

Heat the oil in a heavy-based pan and brown the chicken pieces on all sides. Remove from the pan and cook the onion and garlic until the onion is soft but without colour. Stir in the parsley and return the chicken to the pan.

Put the 450 g/1 lb grapes in a food processor and purée to release the juice. Pour the juice over the chicken and season with salt and white pepper. Bring to the boil, cover with a piece of greaseproof paper and a tight-fitting lid and cook for a further 35-45 minutes until the chicken is tender.

Place the chicken on a hot serving dish and keep hot. Pour the brandy into the sauce. Bring to the boil and, if necessary, boil to reduce the sauce to a thin coating consistency. Add the extra grapes and bring to the boil again. Check the seasoning and pour over the chicken. Sprinkle a little more chopped parsley over just before serving. Serve hot.

134 PRESSED CHICKEN

Preparation time:
25 minutes, plus marinating

Cooking time:
30-40 minutes

Serves 2

Calories:
965 per portion

YOU WILL NEED:
1 × 1 kg/2 lb chicken
3 tablespoons olive oil
1 garlic clove, crushed
1 bay leaf, crumbled
1 sprig of rosemary
salt and pepper
juice of ½ lemon

Cut the chicken in half along the backbone. Remove the backbone and beat the chicken with a mallet as flat as possible. Wash and dry the chicken with absorbent kitchen paper. Place flat in a shallow dish. Mix all the remaining ingredients, except the lemon juice, and pour over the chicken. Leave to marinate for 2-3 hours, turning once.

Oil the base of a heavy frying pan and heat gently. Put in the chicken and press a heavy lid which fits inside the pan down on top of it. Cook over low to moderate heat for 30-40 minutes, until the chicken is golden brown and tender. Transfer to a warm serving dish.

Sprinkle the lemon juice over the chicken together with any juices from the chicken. Serve immediately.

■ COOK'S TIP

If you cannot obtain seedless grapes, take care when puréeing grapes with seeds to release the juice that they are not overprocessed or the sauce will be gritty. Remove the seeds from the grapes used as a garnish. You could use bought grape juice instead; about 450 ml/15 fl oz would be needed.

■ COOK'S TIP

Use poultry scissors or a heavy knife and a mallet to chop the chicken in half. Use a sharp knife and your fingers to prise the meat gently away from the split backbone.

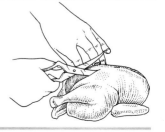

135 CHICKEN MARENGO

Preparation time:
30-40 minutes

Cooking time:
50-55 minutes

Oven temperature:
190 C/375 F/gas 5

Serves 4-6

Calories:
1,059-706 per
portion

YOU WILL NEED:
8-10 tablespoons olive oil
1 × 1.5 kg/3 ½ lb chicken, jointed
350 g/12 oz ripe tomatoes, skinned,
    seeded and chopped
300 ml/10 fl oz dry white wine
2 garlic cloves, crushed
salt and pepper
2 × 5 mm/¼ inch slices bread, crusts
    removed and cut into triangles
4-6 large prawns
4-6 eggs
2 tablespoons chopped parsley

Heat 2-3 tablespoons of oil in a flameproof casserole and fry the chicken until it is golden brown on all sides. Remove from the pan. Pour some of the oil from the pan, if necessary, and add the tomatoes, garlic and white wine. Season to taste, mix well. Replace the chicken in the pan, bring to the boil and cook in a preheated oven for 35-45 minutes or until the chicken is tender. In the meantime, heat another 2-3 tablespoons of oil in a frying pan and fry the bread until golden brown on all sides. Remove from the pan and keep hot. Fry the prawns for 2-3 minutes until cooked through. Keep hot. Heat another 2-3 tablespoons olive oil in a clean pan and fry the eggs.

When the chicken is cooked arrange it on a hot serving dish. If necessary, boil the sauce to reduce it to a thin coating consistency. Check the seasoning and pour over the chicken. Arrange the prawns, eggs and fried croûtons around the sides of the dish. Sprinkle parsley over before serving. Serve hot.

■ COOK'S TIP

This dish is based on one created by Napoleon's chef after the Battle of Marengo, using what ingredients he could find near the battlefield. To emulate the *deep-fried eggs of the original recipe, fry the eggs here on both sides.*

136 DUCK CASSEROLE WITH TAGLIATELLE

Preparation time:
15 minutes

Cooking time:
about 1 hour
45 minutes

Serves 6

Calories:
637 per portion

YOU WILL NEED:
75 g/3 oz butter
½ onion, chopped
½ carrot, chopped
1 celery stick, chopped
1 bay leaf
1 × 1.5 kg/3 ½ lb oven-ready duckling
50 g/2 oz mushrooms, sliced
450 g/1 lb tomatoes, skinned and
    mashed
300 ml/½ pint chicken stock
salt and pepper
300 g/11 oz tagliatelle

Melt the butter in a flameproof casserole, add the onion, carrot, celery and bay leaf and fry gently for 5 minutes. Add the duckling and fry, turning until browned on all sides, then add the mushrooms, tomatoes, stock and salt and pepper to taste. Bring to the boil, lower the heat, cover and simmer for 1½ hours or until the duckling is tender.

Meanwhile, cook the tagliatelle in boiling salted water until just tender (al dente). Drain thoroughly and pile into a warmed serving dish. Cut the duck into serving pieces and arrange on top of the tagliatelle. Keep hot.

Strain the cooking juices and boil until reduced by about half. Pour over the duck and serve immediately.

■ COOK'S TIP

For extra rich tagliatelle, sprinkle it with a little duck cooking juice, 25 g/1 oz melted butter and 65 g/2 ½ oz grated Parmesan; pile the duck pieces on top.

137 HUNTER'S-STYLE CHICKEN

Preparation time:
25-30 minutes

Cooking time:
50-60 minutes

Oven temperature:
190 C/375 F/gas 5

Serves 4

Calories:
794 per portion

YOU WILL NEED:
1 × 1.5 kg/3 ½ lb chicken, jointed
3-4 tablespoons olive oil
50 g/2 oz fat bacon, diced
1 onion, finely chopped
1 garlic clove, crushed
1 teaspoon flour
150 ml/5 fl oz dry white wine
300 ml/10 fl oz chicken stock
4 ripe tomatoes, peeled, seeded and
*   sliced*
1 teaspoon tomato purée
salt and pepper
100 g/4 oz mushrooms, quartered

Heat 2 tablespoons of the oil in a pan and brown the chicken pieces on all sides. Remove from the pan and add the bacon. Cook until golden brown, then remove from the pan. Add more oil if necessary and cook the onion and garlic gently until golden brown. Add the flour and cook together for a few moments, then stir in the white wine, stock, tomato purée and tomato. Bring to the boil and season lightly. Return the chicken and bacon to the casserole. Cover with a tight-fitting lid and cook in a preheated oven for 25-30 minutes. Add the mushrooms and continue cooking for a further 10-15 minutes until the chicken and mushrooms are tender.

Place the chicken pieces on a hot serving dish, cover and keep hot. If necessary, boil the sauce to reduce it to a coating consistency. Pour over the chicken and sprinkle the chopped parsley over just before serving. Serve hot.

138 CHICKEN BAKED WITH PEPPERS

Preparation time:
10 minutes

Cooking time:
50-60 minutes

Oven temperature:
190 C/375 F/gas 5

Serves 4

Calories:
482 per portion

YOU WILL NEED:
4 chicken portions
4 garlic cloves, crushed
4 sprigs rosemary or 1 teaspoon dried
*   rosemary*
4 peppers (see Cook's Tip), cored,
*   seeded and quartered or cut into 8*
2 tablespoons olive oil
salt and pepper
6 tablespoons white wine
Continental parsley, to garnish

Wipe the chicken with absorbent kitchen paper and place in a baking dish. Add the garlic and rosemary.

Place the peppers around the chicken and drizzle over the oil. Sprinkle with salt and pepper.

Pour the wine into the dish, cover and bake in a preheated oven for 50-60 minutes. After 35 minutes remove the cover to brown the chicken.

Place the chicken on a warmed serving dish and surround with peppers. Keep warm. Boil the pan juices and simmer for 2 minutes. Pour over the chicken and peppers and garnish with the parsley.

■ COOK'S TIP

Use 4 chicken breasts or 8 thighs for this recipe. Chicken breasts will only need a total of 25-30 minutes to cook but thighs will need longer.

■ COOK'S TIP

Choose different coloured peppers to give extra colour to this dish. Although the green pepper is just an unripe yellow or red pepper, they all cook at the same rate.

139 HOME-STYLE SAUTEED GUINEA FOWL

Preparation time:
15-20 minutes

Cooking time:
40-45 minutes

Serves 4

Calories:
616 per portion

YOU WILL NEED:
1 × 1.5 kg/3-3 ½ lb guinea fowl, jointed
salt and pepper
50 g/2 oz butter
2-3 tablespoons olive oil
450 g/1 lb tomatoes, skinned, seeded
 and sliced or 1 × 400 g/14 oz can
 tomatoes, drained, seeded and sliced
1 tablespoon chopped parsley

To joint the guinea fowl: place it on a board, breast uppermost, and cut through the skin between the body and the leg. Press the whole leg (the thigh and drumstick) outwards to break the joint. Cut through any flesh, sinew or skin holding the leg to the carcase. Cut through the joint between the thigh and the drumstick. Repeat on the other side. Trim the first two joints away from the wing. Cut the breast away from the wing and break the wing joint in the same way as the leg. Cut through this joint. Cut the breast into two pieces.

Season the guinea fowl with salt and pepper. Heat the butter and oil in a flameproof casserole and brown the pieces of guinea fowl well on all sides over a good heat. Lower the heat, cover with a tight-fitting lid and cook over a gentle heat, turning the pieces of guinea fowl from time to time, for 25-35 minutes or until the bird is tender. Drain off most of the fat from the pan and add the tomatoes. Cook until they thicken slightly and season to taste. Pour into a serving dish, sprinkle over the parsley and serve hot.

▨ COOK'S TIP

Once a game bird, related to the pheasant, guinea fowl have long been reared domestically. They have a flavourful flesh and may be roasted or casseroled.

140 CHICKEN TONNATO

Preparation time:
20 minutes, plus
cooling

Cooking time:
25-35 minutes

Serves 4

Calories:
427 per portion

YOU WILL NEED:
4 chicken breasts, skinned and boned
600 ml/1 pint chicken stock
1 onion, halved
1 celery stick, roughly chopped
salt and pepper
pinch of dried thyme
few parsley stalks
½ bay leaf
150 ml/¼ pint white wine (optional)
450 ml/¾ pint thick mayonnaise
1 × 198 g/7 oz can tuna, drained
6 anchovy fillets, drained
2 tablespoons lemon juice
3 tablespoons drained capers
FOR THE GARNISH
anchovy fillets
capers
tomato slices

Place the chicken, stock, onion, celery, salt and pepper to taste, herbs, wine, if using, and enough water to cover, in a large saucepan. Bring to the boil, then simmer very gently for 20-30 minutes until the chicken is tender and cooked. Remove the chicken from the pan with a slotted spoon and leave to cool.

Purée the mayonnaise, tuna, anchovy fillets, lemon juice and capers in a blender until smooth. Put the cooled chicken breasts on a serving dish and spoon the sauce over them to cover. Garnish with anchovy fillets, capers and tomato slices. Serve immediately.

▨ COOK'S TIP

Use the stock/water in which the chicken breasts were cooked as the basis for a soup. Strain the stock and cook very small pasta in it for pastina in brodo.

141 STUFFED DUCK

Preparation time:
25 minutes

Cooking time:
2-2½ hours

Oven temperature:
180 C/350 F/gas 4

Serves 6

Calories:
960 per portion

YOU WILL NEED:
50 g/2 oz dripping
50 g/2 oz bacon, chopped
1 onion, chopped
225 g/8 oz minced beef
225 g/8 oz minced pork
100 g/4 oz salsiccia a metro
100 g/4 oz rice, cooked
salt and pepper
3 eggs, beaten
1 garlic clove, crushed
1 tablespoon chopped parsley
pinch of grated nutmeg
1 × 1.5 kg/3 ½ lb oven-ready duckling, boned
1-2 tablespoons olive oil
1 rosemary sprig
6-8 tablespoons chicken stock

Melt the dripping in a heavy pan, add the bacon and onion and fry gently 5 minutes. Add the beef, pork and sausage and fry 10 minutes, stirring. Take off the heat, add the rice, then the eggs, garlic, parsley, nutmeg and salt and pepper.

Stuff the duckling with this mixture, then sew up with trussing thread or string. Heat the oil with the rosemary in a roasting tin. Add the duck and brown on all sides, then roast in a preheated oven for 1½-2 hours until the duck is tender, basting occasionally with a little stock. Slice the duck and serve hot, with the cooking juices poured over.

142 ROAST PHEASANT WITH SAGE

Preparation time:
15-20 minutes

Cooking time:
40 minutes

Oven temperature:
190 C/375 F/gas 5

Serves 4

Calories:
618 per portion

YOU WILL NEED:
100 g/4 oz raw ham, chopped
50 g/2 oz bacon, chopped
few sage leaves, chopped
salt and pepper
1 × 1.5 kg/3 ½ lb pheasant, cleaned
4 bacon rashers
sage leaves, to garnish

Mix the ham, bacon and sage together. Sprinkle the inside of the pheasant with salt and pepper, then fill with the ham mixture. Sew up the opening with trussing thread or string, then place the bacon on top and tie with string.

Place the pheasant in an oiled roasting tin and roast in a preheated oven for 40 minutes until tender, basting occasionally with the pan juices.

Remove the thread or string from the pheasant and place on a warmed serving platter. Sprinkle with the cooking juices and garnish with sage leaves. Serve immediately.

▇ COOK'S TIP

Cook the rice in boiling, salted water for 10 minutes only, then drain it thoroughly. The salsiccia a metro (see recipe 117) should be skinned and diced before
being fried with the minced beef and pork.

▇ COOK'S TIP

Parma ham – prosciutto di Parma – is the best known Italian raw ham. Other salted raw hams are San Daniele hams and coppa hams (shoulder cuts).

143 CASSEROLED CHICKEN WITH OLIVES AND ANCHOVIES

Preparation time:
20-25 minutes

Cooking time:
50-55 minutes

Oven temperature:
190 C/375 F/gas 5

Serves 4

Calories:
802 per portion

YOU WILL NEED:
salt and pepper
½ teaspoon powdered bay leaf
4 chicken joints
2-3 tablespoons olive oil
1 large onion, finely chopped
2 garlic cloves, crushed
3 tablespoons brandy
300 ml/10 fl oz dry white wine
12 black olives, pitted and chopped
5-6 anchovy fillets, washed and chopped

Rub a little salt, plenty of pepper and the powdered bay leaf over the chicken joints. Heat the oil in a fireproof casserole and brown the chicken joints on all sides. Remove from the pan and add the onion and garlic. Cook gently until soft and lightly coloured.

Return the chicken to the casserole and pour over the brandy. Raise the heat and boil until the brandy has evaporated, turning the chicken in the brandy to coat it well. Pour on the white wine, mix well and taste to check the seasoning, remembering that when the anchovies are added at the end, they will add salt. Cover with a tight-fitting lid, bring to the boil and transfer to a preheated oven for 30-40 minutes until the chicken is tender. Add the olives and heat through. Just before serving, stir in the anchovies. Arrange the chicken on a hot serving dish, pour the sauce over and serve hot.

144 STUFFED PARTRIDGES

Preparation time:
20 minutes

Cooking time:
40-45 minutes

Oven temperature:
200 C/400 F/gas 6

Serves 4

Calories:
804 per portion

YOU WILL NEED:
4 partridges, with their livers
salt and pepper
100 g/4 oz mushrooms, finely chopped
350 g/12 oz unsmoked streaky bacon rashers
6 juniper berries, crushed
50 g/2 oz butter
4 slices bread, cut into rounds
watercress, to garnish

Wash the partridges and dry well with absorbent kitchen paper. Sprinkle with salt and pepper.

Chop the partridge liver finely and mix with the mushrooms. Reserve 8 slices of bacon and rind and chop the remainder. Mix with the mushrooms and liver, adding the juniper berries, salt and pepper.

Stuff the birds and wrap 2 slices of bacon around each. Place in a roasting tin with the butter. Roast in a preheated oven for 35-40 minutes until the birds are tender. Remove and keep warm.

Heat the pan juices on top of the stove. Fry the bread in the juices until crisp and golden, then place on a warmed dish with the partridges on top, and garnish with watercress. Potato gnocchi (recipe 90) or polenta make good accompaniments.

■ COOK'S TIP

If you find anchovies are rather salty for your taste, soak them in a little milk for 20-30 minutes before you use them. Dry well on absorbent kitchen paper.

■ COOK'S TIP

Juniper is used to flavour game, pâtés and pork (as well as gin). The berries are usually sold dried and will keep for some time.

145 SAUTEED CHICKEN WITH OLIVES

Preparation time: 20 minutes	YOU WILL NEED:
	1 × 1.75 kg/4 lb chicken, in 6 pieces
	seasoned flour for coating
Cooking time: about 1 hour	3 tablespoons olive oil
	1 large onion, chopped
Serves 6	1-2 garlic cloves, crushed
	1 bay leaf
Calories: 656 per portion	150 ml/¼ pint dry white wine
	1 × 400 g/14 oz can peeled tomatoes
	1 tablespoon tomato purée
	12 black olives
	salt and pepper
	parsley, to garnish

Wash and dry the chicken portions and dust lightly with seasoned flour. Heat the oil in a large, heavy-based saucepan and sauté the chicken until golden all over. Transfer to a plate. Add the onion to the pan and sauté for 5 minutes until soft. Add the garlic and bay leaf and sauté for 1 minute. Pour in the wine and simmer for 1-2 minutes, then add the tomatoes and their juice and the tomato purée. Bring to the boil, breaking up the tomatoes if whole, return the chicken to the pan and add the olives. Cover the pan and simmer gently, stirring occasionally, for 45 minutes or until the chicken is tender.

Transfer the chicken to a warm serving dish. Boil the sauce rapidly, uncovered, until reduced by half. Remove the bay leaf, adjust the seasoning if necessary, and pour the sauce over the chicken. Garnish with parsley and serve immediately.

■ COOK'S TIP

Canned pitted olives are a useful storecupboard item. Once opened, transfer the olives to a glass jar. They will keep in the refrigerator for several weeks.

146 CASSEROLED PIGEON WITH PEAS

Preparation time: 15-20 minutes	YOU WILL NEED:
	4 tablespoons olive oil
	100 g/4 oz lean bacon, diced
Cooking time: about 50 minutes	1 onion, chopped
	1 carrot, chopped
Serves 4	1 celery stick, chopped
	1 garlic clove, chopped
Calories: 519 per portion	4 young pigeons, cleaned and halved
	7 tablespoons dry white wine
	350 g/12 oz shelled fresh peas
	pinch of ground cinnamon
	salt and pepper
	450 ml/¾ pint chicken stock

Heat the oil in a flameproof casserole, add the bacon, vegetables and garlic, and fry gently for 10 minutes. Add the pigeons and fry until browned on all sides, turning frequently. Add the wine and cook until it has evaporated.

Add the peas, cinnamon, salt and pepper to taste, and the stock. Cover and simmer for 30 minutes or until the pigeons are tender, basting the pigeons with the cooking liquor occasionally. Serve hot.

■ COOK'S TIP

Pigeons are most likely to be found in the freezer cabinet of the supermarket. Thaw completely before cooking, and use a heavy cook's knife to cut them in half.

147 STUFFED TURKEY BREASTS

Preparation time:
40-45 minutes

Cooking time:
1¼-1½ hours

Oven temperature:
180 C/350 F/gas 4

Serves 4-6

Calories:
549-366 per portion

YOU WILL NEED:
2 eggs
50 g/2 oz grated Parmesan cheese
salt and pepper
3-4 tablespoons olive oil
275 g/10 oz spinach, chopped
pinch nutmeg
2 × 250-275 g/9-10 oz turkey breast
  fillets (see Cook's Tip)
½ teaspoon chopped rosemary
4 rashers lean rindless streaky bacon
25 g/1 oz butter
300 ml/10 fl oz dry white wine

Whisk one of the eggs with half the Parmesan cheese and season well. Heat a scant tablespoon of oil in a 15 cm/6 inch frying pan. Tip in the mixture and spread it to cover the base of the pan. Cook until golden brown, then turn over and cook on the reverse side. Make another omelet. In another pan, heat a tablespoon of oil and cook the spinach over a moderate heat until it softens. Season with salt, pepper and nutmeg.

On each prepared turkey fillet, place an omelet, half the spinach and 2 rashers of streaky bacon. Roll up towards the pointed end and secure with cocktail sticks and string.

Melt the butter and a tablespoon of oil in a flameproof casserole and brown the turkey on all sides. Pour on the wine, season, cover and cook for 1-1¼ hours until the turkey is tender. Take the turkey fillets from the pan and remove the cocktail sticks and strings. Cut into thick slices and arrange on a dish. Pour the cooking liquor over and serve hot.

148 RABBIT WITH OLIVES

Preparation time:
10 minutes

Cooking time:
about 1¼ hours

Serves 4

Calories:
503 per portion

YOU WILL NEED:
7 tablespoons olive oil
1 × 1.25 kg/2 ½ lb rabbit, cleaned and
  cut into serving pieces
2 garlic cloves, chopped
1 rosemary sprig, chopped
200 ml/ ⅓ pint red wine
salt and pepper
6-8 tablespoons chicken stock
2 tomatoes, skinned and mashed
225 g/8 oz black olives, halved and
  stoned

Heat the oil in a flameproof casserole, add the rabbit and sprinkle with the garlic and rosemary. Fry gently until the rabbit is browned on all sides, turning frequently.

Add the wine and salt and pepper to taste. Cover and simmer for 30 minutes, adding a little stock to moisten as necessary.

Add the tomatoes and olives and cook for a further 40 minutes until the rabbit is tender. Serve hot.

■ COOK'S TIP

To prepare turkey fillets, place on a board and with a small knife held parallel to the board, make a cut right through the thickest side. Cut almost through to the other edge right down the length of the fillet, then open it out and flatten it well. Remove the white sinew, which is clearly visible, with the point of a knife.

■ COOK'S TIP

Rabbit pieces are widely available from supermarkets. The mixture of flavouring ingredients here would also go well with chicken pieces.

149 SALMIS OF HARE

Preparation time:
30-40 minutes, plus
marinating

Cooking time:
2¼-2¾ hours

Oven temperature:
190 C/375 F/gas 5

Serves 4-6

Calories:
535-357 per portion

YOU WILL NEED:
1 medium-sized hare, jointed and
   washed
1 × quantity marinade (see Cook's Tip)
50 g/2 oz seasoned flour
50 g/2 oz butter
2 tablespoons olive oil
salt and pepper
2 tablespoons brandy

Place the pieces of hare in a deep bowl with the vegetables, herbs, spices, red wine and vinegar of the marinade. Cover and refrigerate for 24-48 hours, turning the hare from time to time in the liquid.

Remove the hare from the marinade and drain until dry. Coat the hare with seasoned flour. Heat the butter and oil in a fireproof casserole and brown the hare on all sides. Pour all the marinade into the pan and season to taste with salt. Bring to the boil, cover and cook in a preheated oven for about 2 hours until the hare is tender.

Remove the hare from the casserole and place on a hot serving dish. Remove the herbs and spices from the pan and purée the vegetables in the sauce in a food processor or liquidizer. Return to the casserole and adjust the consistency of the sauce and the seasoning, if necessary. Add the brandy, bring to the boil, then pour over the hare and serve hot.

150 CHICKEN BRAISED WITH ONIONS AND PIMENTO

Preparation time:
15 minutes

Cooking time:
1 hour 20 minutes

Serves 4

Calories:
613 per portion

YOU WILL NEED:
3-4 tablespoons olive oil
1 small onion, sliced
2 garlic cloves, crushed
1 × 1.25 kg/2 ½ lb oven-ready chicken,
   cut into serving pieces
1 small piece canned pimento, chopped
salt and pepper
1 tablespoon tomato purée
3-4 tablespoons dry white wine
few rosemary sprigs
6-8 tablespoons chicken stock

Heat the oil in a flameproof casserole, add the onion and garlic and fry gently for 15 minutes. Add the chicken pieces with the pimento and salt and pepper to taste and fry, turning, over moderate heat until browned on all sides.

Mix the tomato purée with a little lukewarm water, then stir into the casserole with the wine. Lower the heat, cover and cook gently for 30 minutes. Chop one of the rosemary sprigs and sprinkle over the chicken. Cook for a further 30 minutes or until the chicken is tender, adding a little of the stock occasionally to moisten.

Serve hot, garnished with the remaining rosemary.

■ COOK'S TIP

Marinades tenderize game and meat and give extra flavour. This is a typical recipe: 1 each carrot, celery stick, large onion, all sliced; 1-2 garlic cloves, crushed;

6-8 parsley stalks; 1 sprig thyme or rosemary; 2 bay leaves; 4 juniper berries; 8 peppercorns; 600 ml/1 pint red wine; 4 tablespoons red wine vinegar.

■ COOK'S TIP

Buy a small can of pimentos and use the left-over pimento, finely chopped, in a pasta sauce, such as the basic Tomato sauce (recipe 81) for extra piquancy.

151 VENISON WITH REDCURRANT SAUCE

Preparation time:
30-35 minutes, plus marinating

Cooking time:
1½-2 hours

Oven temperature:
180 C/350 F/gas 4

Serves 4-6

Calories:
509-340 per portion

YOU WILL NEED:
600-750 g/1 ¼-1 ½ lb venison, diced
1 quantity marinade without vinegar (recipe 149)
100 g/4 oz piece rindless streaky bacon, diced
2 tablespoons olive oil
2-3 tablespoons seasoned flour
salt and pepper
6-8 tablespoons redcurrant jelly
2 tablespoons grappa or brandy

Place the venison and marinade in a bowl, cover and refrigerate for at least 24 hours, turning the venison from time to time. Remove the meat from the marinade and drain until dry.

Heat the oil in a pan and cook the bacon until golden brown. Remove from the pan. Toss the venison in the seasoned flour and brown it on all sides in the hot oil. Add the bacon and the marinade. Season lightly, cover and simmer gently on top of the stove, or cook in a preheated oven for 1½-2 hours.

Remove the venison from the pan, cover and keep hot. Strain the cooking liquor into a clean pan and whisk in 2 tablespoons redcurrant jelly. Boil until the sauce reduces to a thin coating consistency. Pour over the meat and keep hot.

Melt the remaining redcurrant jelly in a pan and whisk until smooth. Add the grappa or brandy and boil for about one minute. Pour into a sauce boat and serve separately.

152 DUCK IN SWEET-SOUR SAUCE

Preparation time:
5 minutes

Cooking time:
1 hour 20 minutes

Serves 4

Calories:
861 per portion

YOU WILL NEED:
4 duck breast portions, completely thawed if frozen
50 g/2 oz butter
1 large onion, peeled and thinly sliced
450 ml/ ¾ pint chicken stock
2 tablespoons wine vinegar
2 tablespoons honey
salt and pepper
50 g/2 oz sultanas
2 tablespoons chopped fresh mint
50 g/2 oz pine nuts
mint leaves, to garnish

Wipe the duck with absorbent kitchen paper. Heat the butter in a large saucepan and fry the duck for about 10 minutes, turning until evenly browned.

Remove the duck from the pan and add the onion. Fry for about 5 minutes until softened. Add the stock, vinegar, honey, salt and pepper. Bring to the boil and add the duck.

Simmer, covered, for 1 hour until very tender. Ten minutes before the end of cooking time add the sultanas, mint and pine nuts.

Remove the duck from the sauce and place in a ,warm serving dish. Skim the fat from the top of the sauce and pour the sauce over the duck. Garnish the dish with mint leaves before serving.

■ COOK'S TIP

For this dish, casseroling or shoulder venison is ideal. It is quite reasonable to buy, the price being comparable with other braising meats. Venison is a very lean meat.

■ COOK'S TIP

Use a large, flattish spoon to skim the fat off the sauce. Potato gnocchi (recipe 90) and a green salad would make good accompaniments for this dish.

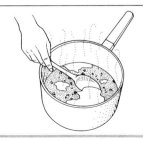

153 RABBIT WITH PEPPERS

Preparation time:
20 minutes

Cooking time:
about 1 hour

Serves 4

Calories:
514 per portion

YOU WILL NEED:
50 g/2 oz butter
50 g/2 oz ham fat or streaky bacon,
  chopped
1 rosemary sprig, chopped
1 kg/2 lb rabbit pieces
1 bay leaf
salt and pepper
7 tablespoons chicken stock
2 tablespoons olive oil
4 green peppers, cored, seeded and
  sliced
4 canned anchovies, soaked in milk,
  drained and mashed
2 garlic cloves, sliced
4 tablespoons white wine vinegar

Melt half the butter in a flameproof casserole, add the ham fat or bacon and rosemary and fry gently for 5 minutes. Add the rabbit, bay leaf and salt and pepper to taste. Fry, turning over high heat until evenly browned, then cover and cook gently for 20 minutes, turning frequently and basting with the stock.

Meanwhile, heat the remaining butter and the oil in a separate pan. Add the peppers, anchovies, garlic and salt and pepper to taste. Cook gently for 20 minutes, adding the vinegar a little at a time during cooking.

Add the pepper mixture to the rabbit and cook gently for a further 30 minutes or until the rabbit is tender. Discard the bay leaf. Serve hot.

154 BOILED CAPON WITH GREEN SAUCE

Preparation time:
20-25 minutes

Cooking time:
2½-3 hours for a capon, 1½-1¾ hours for a large chicken

Serves 6

Calories:
858 per portion

YOU WILL NEED:
1 × 2.5 kg/5 lb capon or large chicken,
  giblets removed, cleaned and trussed
1 carrot, sliced
2 medium onions, quartered
2 cloves stuck into 1 quarter of onion
3-4 parsley stalks
1 bay leaf
1 sprig thyme
6-8 peppercorns
salt and white pepper
1 quantity Green sauce (see Cook's Tip)

Place the capon in a large pan or flameproof casserole. Cover with water and bring slowly to the boil. Remove any scum which rises to the surface. Add the carrot, onions, cloves stuck into a piece of the onion, parsley stalks, bay leaf, thyme and peppercorns and season to taste with salt and pepper.

Bring to the boil, then reduce the heat and simmer gently until the bird is tender. A capon will take 2½-3 hours and a large chicken about 1½ hours. Remove the bird carefully from the pan, allow all the liquid to drain from it and place on a hot serving dish. Whisk the sauce well, pour into a sauce boat and serve separately.

■ COOK'S TIP

Soaking the anchovies in milk before using plumps them up and reduces their saltiness, leaving their true flavour to give a delicious piquancy to this dish.

■ COOK'S TIP

Put 1 small potato, mashed in a bowl. Add 1 crushed garlic clove, 1 small chopped onion, 2 mashed anchovy fillets, 1 tablespoon chopped capers, 1-2 chopped hard-boiled eggs and 2 tablespoons chopped parsley. Beat in 120 ml/4 fl oz olive oil and 3-4 tablespoons red wine vinegar. Season with pepper.

155 CHICKEN CASSEROLED WITH GARLIC AND WINE

Preparation time:
10 minutes

Cooking time:
1 hour 10 minutes

Serves 6

Calories:
526 per portion

YOU WILL NEED:
4 tablespoons olive oil
3 garlic cloves
1 × 1.5 kg/3 lb oven-ready chicken, cut into serving pieces
salt and pepper
500 ml/18 fl oz Vernaccia or other dry white wine
chopped parsley, to garnish

Heat the oil in a flameproof casserole, add the garlic and fry gently until browned. Discard the garlic and add the chicken pieces to the casserole. Fry over high heat until browned on all sides, turning frequently. Add salt and pepper to taste, then add the wine.

Lower the heat, cover and cook gently for 1 hour or until the chicken is tender, stirring occasionally. Serve hot, garnished with parsley.

156 QUAIL WITH PEAS AND HAM

Preparation time:
20-30 minutes

Cooking time:
40-50 minutes

Oven temperature:
190 C/375 F/gas 5

Serves 4

Calories:
403 per portion

YOU WILL NEED:
50 g/2 oz butter
1 tablespoon olive oil
4-8 quail, cleaned and trussed
100 g/4 oz gammon steak, diced
150 ml/5 fl oz dry white wine
1 × 400 g/14 oz can whole tomatoes, drained, seeded and chopped
salt and pepper
350 g/12 oz shelled fresh or frozen peas
150 ml/5 fl oz chicken stock or juice from canned tomatoes

Heat half the butter and the oil in a flameproof casserole and brown the quail on all sides. Remove from the pan and add half the diced gammon. Cook until lightly coloured, return the quail to the pan with the wine and tomatoes. Season to taste and bring to the boil. Cover tightly and cook in a preheated oven for 20-25 minutes until the quail are just tender.

Meanwhile, heat the remainder of the butter in a pan and cook the rest of the gammon until it is golden brown. Add the peas and, if necessary, a little water. Season lightly with salt and pepper. Simmer gently until the peas are tender and all the liquid has evaporated. Keep hot.

Remove the cooked quail from the pan and remove any trussing strings. Place on a hot serving dish and keep hot. Add the pea mixture to the pan and stir well over a gentle heat until the peas are coated with the sauce and are heated through. If necessary, add more liquid to the pan to give a coating consistency. Pile on the dish and serve hot.

■ COOK'S TIP

The white wine in this dish could be replaced by a mixture of lemon juice (from 2 lemons) and water, if liked

■ COOK'S TIP

If you are using fresh peas, choose young tender ones and add sufficient water to soften them but allow it almost to boil away by the time they are cooked. Frozen

peas should need almost no water and will take only a few minutes to cook. Quail are very meaty little birds and you may find 1 is enough per person.

PIZZAS & RICE

Pizzas are believed to have been invented by frugal Neapolitans to use up bread dough. Today, they are one of the world's most popular fast foods. Italian rice, too, has special qualities of flavour and cookability which give it great appeal at home and abroad. Classic recipes and new ideas for these great foods are included here.

157 PIZZA WITH ONIONS AND EGGS

Preparation time:	YOU WILL NEED:
20-25 minutes	4-5 tablespoons olive oil
	750 g-1 kg/1½-2 lb onions, finely sliced
Cooking time:	salt and pepper
40-45 minutes	1 quantity Basic pizza dough (recipe
	159)
Oven temperature:	2-3 hardboiled eggs, sliced
200 C/475 F/gas 9	1-2 tablespoons chopped parsley
Serves 4	
Calories:	
588 per portion	

Heat 3-4 tablespoons oil in a pan and cook the onions over a moderate heat until they are soft and lightly coloured. Season well with salt and pepper.

Roll the dough out to 2 × 30 cm/12 inch circles and place on a baking tray. Spread the cooked onions over the surface and bake in a preheated oven for 20-30 minutes until the pizzas are golden brown.

Arrange the slices of hardboiled egg on the tops, sprinkle the remainder of the oil over and return to the oven for a further 2-3 minutes. Sprinkle chopped parsley over just before serving.

158 TWO-CHEESE PIZZA

Preparation time:	YOU WILL NEED:
20 minutes, plus rising	15 g/½ oz fresh yeast
	2 tablespoons warm water
	225 g/8 oz plain flour
Cooking time:	salt
20-25 minutes	2 tablespoons olive oil
	3 tablespoons milk
Oven temperature:	FOR THE TOPPING
220 C/425 F/gas 7; then	4 tablespoons olive oil
180 C/350 F/gas 4	1 × 400 g/14 oz can tomatoes, drained
	salt and pepper
Serves 4	1 tablespoon chopped fresh basil
Calories:	1 teaspoon dried oregano
541 per portion	175 g/6 oz Mozzarella or Bel Paese cheese, sliced
	4 tablespoons grated Parmesan cheese

Make the pizza base as for Basic pizza dough (recipe 159), adding the olive oil and milk with the yeast mixture.

Turn the risen dough on to a floured surface and divide into 2 or 4 pieces, depending on the size of pizzas required. Knead each piece lightly and place on well oiled aluminium pie plates. With floured knuckles, press out the dough to cover the base of the plates and reach 1 cm/½ inch up the side. Brush with oil, cover with chopped tomatoes and season. Sprinkle with basil and oregano. Place the cheese on top and sprinkle with Parmesan. Sprinkle oil over each pizza. Leave to rise in a warm place for 30 minutes. Bake in a preheated oven 15 minutes. Reduce the heat and bake for another 5-10 minutes.

■ COOK'S TIP

This pizza recipe can be served hot or cold. If it is to be served cold, do not return it to the oven after the hardboiled eggs have been arranged on the top.

■ COOK'S TIP

Extra toppings which could be added on this pizza are anchovy fillets, olives, sliced mushrooms or sliced Italian sausage.

159 BASIC PIZZA DOUGH

Preparation time:
10 minutes, plus
kneading and rising

Makes: see Cook's
Tip

Total calories:
1,373

YOU WILL NEED:
25 g/1 oz fresh yeast
300 ml/ ½ pint tepid water
400 g/14 oz strong plain flour plus
*   extra for working the dough*
1 teaspoon salt

Blend the yeast with part of the tepid water. Sieve the flour and salt into a large mixing bowl. Make a well in the centre and pour in the yeast mixture and the remaining tepid water. Using your hand, and with a circular movement, gradually work the flour into the liquid moving from the centre of the well outwards to form a sticky, elastic dough.

Turn the dough out on to a floured working surface and knead it well, adding more flour if necessary, until it stops sticking to your knuckles and the working surface. Knead it well for approximately 10 minutes until it becomes smooth and elastic.

At this stage, if you are making more than one pizza, divide the dough into the required number of pieces and knead each one into a ball. Sprinkle the bottom of the mixing bowl with flour and leave the dough to rise, covering the bowl with a cloth, for approximately 1 hour. The time required will depend on the warmth of the kitchen. The dough is ready for rolling out when it has doubled in size.

■ COOK'S TIP

This amount of dough can be shaped into two large round pizzas, approx. 30 cm/12 in. in diameter, one large rectangular pizza, or four individual pizzas approx. 20
cm/8 in. in diameter. Pizza tins will help you to shape the pizza better than simple baking trays. The dough is spread thin – about 5 mm/ ¼ inch.

160 PIZZA WITH FISHERMAN'S TOPPING

Preparation time:
20-25 minutes

Cooking time:
about 50 minutes

Oven temperature:
240 C/475 F/gas 9

Serves 4

Calories:
457 per portion

YOU WILL NEED:
225 g/8 oz fresh mussels, cleaned
olive oil
2 garlic cloves, chopped
100 g/4 oz squid, cleaned, cut in pieces
1 × 400 g/14 oz can chopped tomatoes
salt and pepper
225 g/8 oz cleaned, shelled clams
100 g/4 oz cleaned fresh prawns
1 quantity Basic pizza dough (recipe
*   159)*
small bunch of parsley, chopped

Put the mussels in a large pan over the heat, cover, and toss them occasionally to allow all the mussels to open. Discard any which have not opened. Strain and reserve the liquid.

Cover the bottom of a frying pan with olive oil and when it is hot, but not smoking, add the garlic and fry gently until golden. Add the squid and fry gently for 5 minutes, then remove with a slotted spoon. Add the tomatoes, a tablespoon of the juice from the mussels and salt to taste. Simmer gently for about 30 minutes, adding the clams and the prawns 10 minutes before the end. Add the mussels in their shells and the squid and allow to heat through.

Meanwhile, bake the pizza without the topping at the top of a preheated oven for about 15 minutes, until it is well risen. Remove from the oven and arrange the seafood on top. Sprinkle generously with pepper and parsley.

■ COOK'S TIP

Scrub the mussels well to remove any seaweed or other impurities on the shells and pull out the byssus from each mussel (the tuft of silky filament).

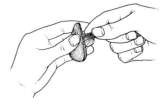

161 PIZZA WITH PEPPERS

Preparation time:
10 minutes

Cooking time:
20-25 minutes

Oven temperature:
240 C/475 F/gas 9

Serves 4

Calories:
425 per portion

YOU WILL NEED:
2 garlic cloves
2 large red peppers
1 quantity Basic pizza dough (recipe 159)
salt
1 teaspoon crushed oregano
2 tablespoons olive oil

Peel and finely chop the garlic. Wash, dry and cut the peppers into very thin rings of approximately 3 mm/⅛ inch, discarding the seeds. Arrange the slices of peppers on top of the pizza, sprinkle with the chopped garlic, salt and oregano and pour the oil over the top.

Bake at the top of a preheated oven for 20-25 minutes, until the pizza has risen and the peppers are cooked.

162 PIZZA WITH TUNA TOPPING

Preparation time:
10 minutes

Cooking time:
35-40 minutes

Oven temperature:
240 C/475 F/gas 9

Serves 4

Calories:
495 per portion

YOU WILL NEED:
1 × 400 g/14 oz can tomatoes
6 black olives
1 small onion
olive oil
salt and pepper
1 × 198 g/7 oz can tuna, drained and flaked
1 quantity Basic pizza dough (recipe 159)

Crush or roughly chop the tomatoes. Stone the olives and cut each one into three or four pieces. Finely chop the onion.

Coat the bottom of a large frying pan with olive oil and gently fry the onion until it is transparent. Add the tomatoes and simmer gently, adding salt to taste, until the sauce becomes denser. Add the tuna and continue to cook for another five minutes. Allow the sauce to cool.

Spread the sauce over the pizza, sprinkle generously with freshly ground black pepper and decorate with the olives. Add a little olive oil.

Bake at the top of a preheated oven for approximately 20 minutes, until the pizza is well risen and the border is golden brown.

■ COOK'S TIP

Black olives and capers can be added and the oregano omitted if preferred. If using oregano, be careful not to add too much as it can give the pizza a bitter flavour.

■ COOK'S TIP

One or two crushed anchovy fillets may be added to the sauce to give it a stronger flavour. Look for ready-pitted olives, available in cans and jars.

163 TOMATO AND ANCHOVY PIZZA

Preparation time:
20-25 minutes, plus rising

Cooking time:
55-65 minutes

Oven temperature:
200 C/400 F/gas 6

Serves 4-6

Calories:
693-462 per portion

YOU WILL NEED:
7 tablespoons olive oil
450 g/1 lb onions, sliced
salt and pepper
450 g/1 lb tomatoes, chopped
1 quantity Basic pizza dough (recipe 159)
100 g/4 oz canned anchovy fillets, drained or cut in half lengthways
100 g/4 oz black olives, halved and stoned
few garlic cloves, peeled and slivered
1 tablespoon chopped basil

Heat 3 tablespoons oil in a heavy pan, add the onions and fry gently for 10 minutes. Season and remove from the heat.

Simmer the tomatoes with salt and pepper to taste for 10-15 minutes until reduced to a pulp; strain.

Knead the dough until smooth and elastic, then flatten with a rolling pin and roll out to a 30 cm/12 inch circle, 1 cm/½ inch thick. Place the circle in a shallow baking tin to fit. Leave to rise in a warm place for 20 minutes.

Spread the onions and tomato pulp over the dough. Arrange the anchovy fillets and olive halves on top. Add slivers of garlic according to taste, then sprinkle with the basil and remaining oil. Bake in a preheated oven for 35-40 minutes.

■ COOK'S TIP

This is a thicker-style pizza, to be served in fat slices. A moderately hot, rather than a hot oven, cooks the thicker base evenly.

164 FOUR SEASONS PIZZA

Preparation time:
15 minutes

Cooking time:
20-25 minutes (excluding sauce)

Oven temperature:
220 C/425 F/gas 7

Serves 4

Calories:
631 per portion

YOU WILL NEED:
2 tablespoons oil
1 garlic clove, crushed
100 g/4 oz button mushrooms, sliced
1 tablespoon chopped parsley
1-2 teaspoons capers
50 g/2 oz peeled prawns
2 rashers streaky bacon, rinded and chopped
2 tablespoons sweetcorn
1 quantity Basic pizza dough (recipe 159)
Tomato sauce (see Cook's Tip)
100 g/4 oz Mozzarella cheese, diced
2 tomatoes, sliced
4 black olives, stoned and halved
1 teaspoon dried mixed herbs

Heat the oil in a pan, add the garlic and mushrooms and cook for 2 minutes. Stir in the parsley and leave to cool.

Mix the capers and prawns together. Mix the bacon and sweetcorn together.

Roll out the dough. Spread the Tomato sauce over the base and sprinkle with the cheese. Using a palette knife, gently mark the pizza into quarters.

Arrange the mushrooms on one quarter, the prawns on another, sprinkle the bacon and sweetcorn on the third quarter, and arrange the tomatoes and olives on the last quarter. Sprinkle the herbs all over. Slide the pizza on to a hot baking sheet and bake in a preheated oven for 15-20 minutes.

■ COOK'S TIP

For Tomato sauce: cook 1 crushed garlic clove, 2 chopped shallots in oil 5 minutes. Add 100 g/4 oz chopped canned tomatoes, 65 ml/2 ½ fl oz white wine, *pinch mixed herbs, seasoning. Cook fairly rapidly for 10-15 minutes until thickened.*

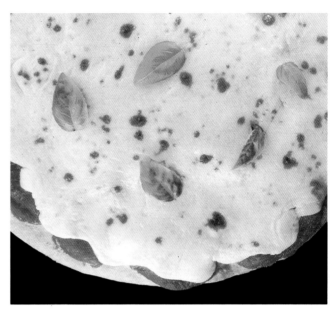

165 ARTICHOKE AND MUSHROOM PIZZA

Preparation time:
15 minutes

Cooking time:
15-20 minutes

Oven temperature:
220 C/425 F/gas 7

Serves 4

Calories:
538 per portion

YOU WILL NEED:

1 quantity Basic pizza dough (recipe 159)
2 tablespoons tomato purée
4-6 tomatoes, skinned and sliced
2 tablespoons chopped basil
2 tablespoons chopped oregano
1 × 397 g/14 oz can artichoke hearts, drained and sliced
50 g/2 oz button mushrooms, thinly sliced
3 tablespoons olive oil
25 g/1 oz Parmesan cheese, grated
25 g/1 oz Cheddar cheese, grated

Roll out the dough. Spread the tomato purée thinly over the base. Arrange the tomatoes on top and sprinkle with the herbs. Place the artichokes and mushrooms on top and drizzle over the oil. Sprinkle with the cheeses.

Slide the pizza on to a hot baking sheet and bake in a preheated oven for 15-20 minutes, until golden. Serve immediately.

166 PIZZA MARGHERITA

Preparation time:
10-15 minutes

Cooking time:
20-25 minutes

Oven temperature:
240 C/475 F/gas 9

Serves 4

Calories:
610 per portion

YOU WILL NEED:

1 × 400 g/14 oz can tomatoes
225 g/8 oz mozzarella cheese
8-10 fresh basil leaves
1 quantity Basic pizza dough (recipe 159)
salt
2 tablespoons grated Parmesan cheese
2 tablespoons olive oil
whole basil leaves, to garnish

Crush or roughly chop the tomatoes. Roughly chop the mozzarella cheese into small pieces. Wash and dry the basil leaves.

Spoon the tomatoes over the pizza and sprinkle them with salt. Sprinkle the pieces of mozzarella cheese evenly over the pizza. Break the basil leaves into small pieces and distribute them evenly over the pizza, then pour on the oil.

Bake at the top of a preheated oven for 20-25 minutes, until the pizza is well risen and the cheese has melted and started to turn golden. Garnish the cooked pizza with whole fresh basil leaves, if liked.

■ COOK'S TIP

Good quality tomato purée is available in jars and tubes. Once opened, both kinds should be kept in the refrigerator.

■ COOK'S TIP

This is probably the most famous pizza topping both in Italy and abroad. Choose cans of ready-chopped tomatoes to save time.

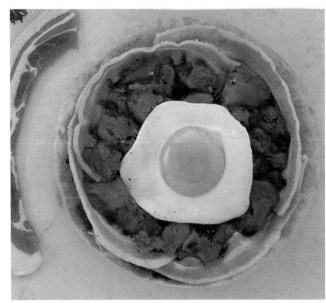

167 BAKED VEGETABLE PIZZA

Preparation time:
15 minutes, plus
cooling

Cooking time:
25-30 minutes

Oven temperature:
220 C/425 F/gas 7

Serves 4

Calories:
619 per portion

YOU WILL NEED:
100 g/4 oz mangetout peas
50 g/2 oz French beans
50 g/2 oz baby carrots, sliced
salt and pepper
4 canned artichoke hearts, drained
25 g/1 oz butter
25 g/1 oz flour
150 ml/¼ pint milk
2 tablespoons cream
25 g/1 oz Parmesan cheese, grated
50 g/2 oz Cheddar cheese, grated
pinch of dried mixed herbs
2 egg yolks
*1 quantity Basic pizza dough (recipe
159)*

Blanch the mangetout peas, beans and carrots (see Cook's Tip).
Drain, cool, then cut the beans and mangetouts in half and slice
the artichokes. Mix all the vegetables together.

Melt the butter in a pan, add the flour and cook for 2
minutes, without browning. Gradually add the milk, bring to
the boil, stirring, and cook for 2 minutes. Remove from the
heat, stir in the cream, Parmesan cheese, half the Cheddar
cheese, herbs and egg yolks. Stir in the vegetables.

Roll out the dough, making the edge at least twice as thick
as the rest and 2.5 cm/1 inch high. Spoon the sauce into the
centre and sprinkle over the remaining Cheddar cheese.

Slide the pizza on to a hot baking sheet and bake in a
preheated oven for 15-20 minutes, until golden.

168 PIZZA WITH BACON AND EGG TOPPING

Preparation time:
10 minutes

Cooking time:
about 20 minutes

Oven temperature:
240 C/475 F/gas 9

Serves 4

Calories:
578 per portion

YOU WILL NEED:
*1 quantity Basic pizza dough (recipe
159)*
1 × 227 g/8 oz can tomatoes
salt and pepper
8 rindless rashers lean streaky bacon
2 tablespoons olive oil
4 fresh eggs

Make four individual pizzas with the dough.

Crush the tomatoes or blend them briefly in a liquidizer and
spread them over the pizzas, taking care not to cover the
borders. Sprinkle them with salt and pepper. Arrange the
rashers of bacon around the inside of the borders and pour the
oil over the top.

Bake the pizzas at the top of a preheated oven for approximately 15 minutes. Take the pizzas out of the oven and break
an egg on to the middle of each one. Put them back in the oven
until the whites of the eggs have set but the yolks are still
liquid, which takes about another 10 minutes.

■ COOK'S TIP

*To blanch the vegetables,
trim them, drop into boiling
salted water and cook for
just 3 minutes.*

■ COOK'S TIP

*The eggs must be very fresh
so that they will stay in the
centre of the pizza. (Fresh
eggs are much less liquid
than those which have been
around for a few days.)*

169 DOUBLE-DECKER PIZZA

Preparation time:
15 minutes, plus
rising

Cooking time:
about 25 minutes

Oven temperature:
240 C/475 F/gas 9

Serves 4

Calories:
696 per portion

YOU WILL NEED:
1 quantity Potato dough (recipe 180)
4 hard-boiled eggs
150 g/5 oz lean cooked ham
225 g/8 oz mozzarella cheese
225 g/8 oz canned or fresh tomatoes
salt and pepper
½ teaspoon crushed oregano
1 tablespoon olive oil

Make the dough, divide it into two parts and leave it to rise until it has doubled in size. Cut the hard-boiled eggs into wedges and chop the cooked ham and mozzarella into small pieces. Crush or slice the tomatoes.

Press the dough out into two circles about 25-30 cm/10-12 inches in diameter, making one slightly larger than the other. Place the larger one on a baking tray.

Put the chopped ham and mozzarella on to the pizza, leaving a 1.5 cm/¾ inch border. Arrange the wedges of egg on top, sprinkle with salt and pepper. Dampen the border with a little water. Cover the pizza with the second circle of dough, fold the border of the bottom circle up over the top one and pinch them well together. Make one or two small holes in the top to allow steam to escape. Leave the pizza to rise for 30 minutes.

Spread the tomatoes over the top, sprinkle with oregano and a little salt and pour on the olive oil. Bake at the top of a preheated oven for approximately 25 minutes.

170 PIZZA WITH AUBERGINE TOPPING

Preparation time:
15 minutes, plus
salting the
aubergines

Cooking time:
25-30 minutes

Oven temperature:
240 C/475 F/gas 9

Serves 4

Calories:
603 per portion

YOU WILL NEED:
2 medium aubergines
coarse sea salt
olive oil
1 × 227 g/8 oz can tomatoes
2 garlic cloves
225 g/8 oz mozzarella cheese
1 quantity Basic pizza dough (recipe 159)

Wash, dry and cut the aubergines into cubes of approximately 1.5 cm/¾ in. Do not peel them. Put the cubes in a colander with layers of coarse sea salt, place a weight on top and leave them for approximately 30 minutes to allow the salt to draw the bitterness out of the aubergines. Rinse off the salt and squeeze the aubergines to remove as much liquid as possible.

Fry the cubes in olive oil and drain them on absorbent kitchen paper. Crush the tomatoes, or blend them briefly in a liquidizer. Peel and finely chop the garlic. Roughly grate the mozzarella cheese. Spread the tomatoes on the pizza, sprinkle with garlic. Cover the pizza with the aubergine cubes and top with the mozzarella cheese. Pour 2 tablespoons olive oil over the top. Bake at the top of a preheated oven for 20-25 minutes.

■ COOK'S TIP

Different fillings can be invented, making use of the contents of your storecupboard or fridge, and olives can be added.

■ COOK'S TIP

Do not add any salt to the pizza topping as the aubergines remain slightly salty after being rinsed and squeezed out.

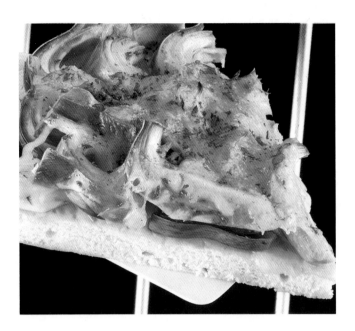

171 PIZZA WITH ARTICHOKE TOPPING

Preparation time:
15-20 minutes, plus soaking

Cooking time:
25-30 minutes

Oven temperature:
240 C/475 F/gas 9

Serves 4

Calories:
629 per portion

YOU WILL NEED:
4 globe artichokes
juice of ½ lemon
225 g/8 oz Emmental cheese
1 quantity Basic pizza dough (recipe 159)
salt and pepper
2 tablespoons olive oil

Prepare the artichokes by pulling off the tough outside leaves until those underneath are whitish. Cut off the top third of the artichokes to eliminate the tips of the leaves. Peel the stalk, leaving the tender core. Rub the prepared artichokes with lemon juice and leave them in cold water and lemon juice for approximately 15 minutes.

Drain the artichokes well and cut them lengthways into very thin wedges of approximately 3 mm/⅛ in, and the stalks into very thin strips. Grate the cheese. Arrange the artichokes on top of the pizza, sprinkle with salt, pepper and grated cheese. Pour the oil over the top.

Bake at the top of a preheated oven for 25-30 minutes, until the pizza has risen and the cheese is golden brown.

172 ROMAN-STYLE PIZZA

Preparation time:
10 minutes

Cooking time:
about 20 minutes

Oven temperature:
240 C/475 F/gas 9

Serves 4

Calories:
602 per portion

YOU WILL NEED:
1 × 227 g/8 oz can tomatoes
225 g/8 oz mozzarella cheese
6 anchovy fillets
1 quantity Basic pizza dough (recipe 159)
salt
2 tablespoons olive oil

Crush the tomatoes or blend them briefly in a liquidizer. Roughly grate the mozzarella cheese. Cut the anchovy fillets into slivers.

Spread the tomato over the pizza and sprinkle it with a little salt and the grated mozzarella. Arrange the pieces of anchovy fillet on the top and pour the oil over the pizza.

Bake at the top of a preheated oven for approximately 20 minutes, until the pizza has risen well and the mozzarella has melted. The border should be golden brown.

■ COOK'S TIP

The use of lemon when preparing the artichokes removes their bitter taste, and prevents them turning brown. Cheese slices can be used instead of grated.

■ COOK'S TIP

This pizza is called alla Romana *in Naples and* alla Napoletana *in Rome. It is one of the best-known pizza toppings.*

173 INDIVIDUAL PINE NUT PIZZAS

Preparation time:
20 minutes

Cooking time:
45 minutes

Oven temperature:
200 C/400 F/gas 6

Serves 2

Calories:
836 per portion

YOU WILL NEED:
3 tablespoons olive oil
225 g/8 oz onions, thinly sliced
1 small red pepper, cored, seeded and
    sliced
salt and pepper
1 quantity Calzoni dough (recipe 177)
100 g/4 oz Bel Paese
50 g/2 oz stuffed green olives, sliced
25 g/1 oz pine nuts
2 teaspoons grated Parmesan cheese
2 teaspoons chopped fresh basil

Heat the oil in a frying pan, add the onions and cook for 5 minutes. Add the red pepper, salt and pepper and cook for 5 minutes until the onions are softened and lightly coloured. Set aside to cool.

Knead the dough briefly on a lightly floured surface. Divide in half and roll out each half to a 20 cm/8 inch round. Place on a greased baking sheet.

Spread the onion mixture evenly over each base. Slice the Bel Paese thinly and arrange over the top. Sprinkle with olives and pine nuts and top with Parmesan cheese. Sprinkle basil over the top.

Bake in a preheated oven for 35 minutes until the cheese has melted and turned golden brown.

174 YEAST-FREE PIZZA

Preparation time:
20 minutes

Cooking time:
45 minutes

Oven temperature:
200 C/400 F/gas 6

Serves 4

Calories:
404 per portion

YOU WILL NEED:
175 g/6 oz wholewheat self-raising flour
salt and pepper
2 teaspoons dried oregano
50 g/2 oz soft margarine
6 tablespoons natural yogurt
450 g/1 lb tomatoes, skinned and sliced
1 large onion, sliced
2 garlic cloves, crushed
225 g/8 oz button mushrooms, sliced
2 peppers, cored, seeded and sliced
100 g/4 oz Edam cheese, grated
10 black olives, pitted

Mix together the flour, salt, pepper and 1 teaspoon oregano and mix in the margarine and yogurt. Form the mixture into a ball and knead it lightly until smooth. Roll out the dough on a lightly-floured board and use it to line a 25 cm/10 inch greased flan ring placed on a greased baking sheet. Line with grease-proof paper and fill with dried baking beans. Bake in a pre-heated oven for 15 minutes.

Meanwhile, put the tomatoes, remaining oregano, onion and garlic into a pan, season, stir well and bring to the boil. Boil for 20 minutes, stirring once, until the mixture is like a thick sauce. Taste and adjust the seasoning.

Spread the tomato mixture over the pizza. Arrange the mushrooms in a single layer, then the pepper rings on top. Sprinkle the cheese over and garnish with the black olives. Return to the oven and bake for a further 10-15 minutes, or until the cheese is brown and bubbling. Serve hot.

■ COOK'S TIP

These individual pizzas may be frozen before being baked. Open freeze them, then wrap with freezer film when they are firm. Cook from frozen on a greased baking sheet, allowing an extra 10 minutes' cooking time.

■ COOK'S TIP

To give this yeast-free pizza added colour, use 1 red and 1 green pepper. If the topping seems a little tart, add 1 teaspoon soft light brown sugar.

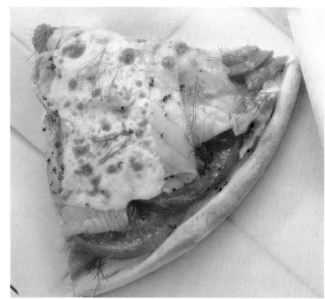

175 EASTER PIZZA

Preparation time:
30 minutes, plus
rising and proving

Cooking time:
25-30 minutes

Oven temperature:
230 C/450 F/gas 8

Serves 8-10

Calories:
641-513 per portion

YOU WILL NEED:
3 eggs
75 g/3 oz grated Parmesan cheese
75 g/3 oz grated pecorino cheese
salt
1 quantity Basic pizza dough (recipe 159), unrisen
125 ml/4 fl oz olive oil
150 g/5 oz strong white flour
180-225 g/6-8 oz salami
1-2 hardboiled eggs, sliced
a little extra olive oil

Beat the eggs and the cheeses together and season with salt. Knead the pizza dough well and press out into a small circle. Pour some of the olive oil and flour into the centre. Fold over the edges, press out into a circle again and repeat the process until all the oil and flour have been incorporated. Knead until smooth. Press out into a larger circle and place the egg mixture in the centre. Fold over and knead well until it is incorporated into the dough. Place in an oiled bowl, cover and keep in a warm place for 1-1½ hours until doubled in size.

Turn out on to a board, knead into a circle and place in a greased 25 cm/10 inch cake tin. Cover and leave to prove until doubled in size. Bake in a preheated oven for 20-30 minutes until it sounds hollow when tapped. Turn out on to a baking tray and return to the oven, upside down, for a few minutes until golden brown. Arrange the salami and hardboiled eggs on top. Sprinkle olive oil over the eggs and return to the oven for a few minutes to warm through.

176 SMOKED SALMON AND DILL PIZZA

Preparation time:
10 minutes

Cooking time:
15-20 minutes

Oven temperature:
220 C/425 F/gas 7

Serves 4

Calories:
536 per portion

YOU WILL NEED:
1 quantity Basic pizza dough (recipe 159)
3 Marmande or Provence tomatoes, skinned and sliced
175 g/6 oz smoked salmon, thinly sliced
1 tablespoon chopped dill
1 tablespoon chopped parsley
100 g/4 oz Mozzarella cheese, sliced

Roll out the dough. Arrange the tomatoes on the pizza base and lay the salmon on top. Sprinkle with the herbs and cover with the cheese.

Slide the pizza on to a hot baking sheet and bake at once in a preheated oven for 15-20 minutes, until golden. Serve immediately.

■ COOK'S TIP

If this pizza is too large for your requirements, you can make a half quantity and bake it in an 18-20 cm/7-8 in. tin. However, you must use the same amount of yeast in the pizza dough as is given for the full quantity.

■ COOK'S TIP

This is a good special occasion pizza. For a less expensive variation, use peeled prawns instead of salmon.

177 CALZONI

Preparation time:
30 minutes, plus
rising

Cooking time:
12-15 minutes

Serves 2

Calories:
663 per portion

YOU WILL NEED:
1 teaspoon dried yeast
½ teaspoon sugar
50 ml/2 fl oz warm water
100 g/4 oz strong plain flour
salt and pepper
1 tablespoon olive oil
oil for deep frying
4 thin slices ham
100 g/4 oz Mozzarella cheese
8 sprigs fresh marjoram
olive oil

Sprinkle the yeast and sugar over the warm water and leave for about 10 minutes until frothy.

Place the flour and half a teaspoon salt in a bowl. Stir in the oil and the yeast liquid and mix to a soft dough. Knead on a lightly floured surface for about 5 minutes. Place the dough in an oiled polythene bag, loosely tied, and leave in a warm place for about 40 minutes, until doubled in size.

Knead the dough briefly until firm and divide into eight pieces. Roll each piece thinly to a 12 cm/5 inch round. Place half a slice of ham on each round with a slice of Mozzarella cheese, a sprig of marjoram (or ½ teaspoon dried marjoram), salt, pepper and a drizzle of olive oil. Fold the dough over and press the edges to seal.

Heat the oil to 180 C/350 F or until a cube of bread browns in 30 seconds. Fry the calzoni, in two or three batches, for 4-5 minutes, until golden brown.

Drain on absorbent kitchen paper and serve warm.

■ COOK'S TIP

*These turnovers will keep
warm in the oven for up to
30 minutes without spoiling.
Serve two per person for a
starter or four each for a
main course.*

178 WHOLEWHEAT PIZZA

Preparation time:
20 minutes, plus
rising

Cooking time:
35 minutes

Oven temperature:
200 C/400 F/gas 6

Serves 6

Calories:
320 per portion

YOU WILL NEED:
15 g/½ oz fresh yeast
½ teaspoon sugar (see Cook's Tip)
6-7 tablespoons warm milk (see Cook's Tip)
25 g/1 oz butter
225 g/8 oz seasoned wholewheat flour
1 tablespoon olive oil
1 onion, chopped
2 streaky bacon rashers
75 g/3 oz cooked ham, chopped
450 g/1 lb cooked spinach, drained
pinch of nutmeg
garlic salt
225 g/8 oz tomatoes, sliced
100 g/4 oz Mozzarella cheese, sliced
¼ teaspoon dried oregano

Rub the butter into the flour. Make a well in the centre and pour in the yeast mixture. Stir well until the mixture forms a ball. Knead 5 minutes, then place in an oiled polythene bag and leave in a warm place for 1 hour until doubled in size.

Heat the oil in a small pan and sauté the onion and bacon 5 minutes. Add the cooked ham. Cool. Season the spinach with nutmeg and garlic salt.

Knead the dough again for 1 minute. Roll out to a 28 cm/11 inch round and place on an oiled baking sheet. Cover with the spinach and bacon, onion and ham. Top with the sliced tomatoes and cheese and sprinkle over the oregano. Bake in a pre-heated oven for 25 minutes.

■ COOK'S TIP

*Blend the fresh yeast in the
warm milk, or dissolve the
sugar in the warm milk and
sprinkle the dried yeast on
top. Leave the yeast in a
warm place for 10 minutes.*

179 PIZZA WITH POTATO TOPPING

Preparation time:
10 minutes

Cooking time:
20-25 minutes

Oven temperature:
240 C/475 F/gas 9

Serves 4

Calories:
489 per portion

YOU WILL NEED:
4 medium potatoes
*1 quantity Basic pizza dough (recipe
  159)*
olive oil
salt
dried or fresh rosemary

Peel the potatoes and cut them into very thin slices of no more than 3 mm/⅛ inch thick. Arrange these slices on the top of the pizza, overlapping them slightly. Brush the potatoes well with olive oil, sprinkle with salt and rosemary.

Bake at the top of a preheated oven for approximately 20-25 minutes, until the pizza has risen and the potatoes are cooked.

180 POTATO DOUGH CALZONI

Preparation time:
20-25 minutes, plus
rising

Cooking time:
about 25 minutes

Oven temperature:
240 C/475 F/gas 9

Serves 4

Calories:
711 per portion

YOU WILL NEED:
FOR POTATO DOUGH
150 g/5 oz cooked, sieved potato
*400 g/14 oz strong plain flour plus
  extra for working the dough*
1 teaspoon salt
25 g/1 oz fresh yeast
350 ml/12 fl oz tepid water
FOR THE FILLING
100 g/4 oz lean cooked ham, cubed
225 g/8 oz mozzarella cheese, cubed
225 g/8 oz ricotta cheese
1 teaspoon chopped fresh basil
2 eggs, beaten
salt and pepper

Prepare the dough as for pizzas (see recipe 159) and leave to rise. Mix all the filling ingredients together, adding salt and pepper to taste.

When the dough has doubled in size (about 1 hour), divide it into eight pieces and press each one out into a circle, approximately 15 cm/6 inch in diameter. Divide the filling between the circles of dough. Moisten the edges of the circles with a little water and fold each one over to form a semi-circle, pressing the edges down well and sealing them. Brush the calzoni with a little beaten egg.

Bake at the top of a preheated oven for approximately 25 minutes, until they are well risen and golden brown.

■ COOK'S TIP

If the potatoes do not brown sufficiently in the oven you can always put the pizza under the grill for a few minutes.

■ COOK'S TIP

Calzoni can be fried instead of baked in the oven. Omit the egg glazing and fry in hot, deep oil for approximately 4-5 minutes on each side. Drain the *calzoni well on kitchen paper and serve immediately. Fried calzoni are softer and lighter than the baked variety as they do not form a crust.*

181 HEART-SHAPED PIZZA

Preparation time:
35 minutes

Cooking time:
45 minutes

Oven temperature:
200 C/400 F/gas 6

Serves 2

Calories:
540 per portion

YOU WILL NEED:
1 × 225 g/8 oz can tomatoes
2 teaspoons dried oregano
1 garlic clove, crushed
1 teaspoon sugar
salt and pepper
1 quantity Calzoni dough (recipe 177)
100 g/4 oz Mozzarella cheese
5 canned artichoke hearts, drained and
  halved
10 anchovy fillets
1 tablespoon chopped fresh parsley

Place the tomatoes in a saucepan with 1 teaspoon oregano, the garlic, sugar, salt and pepper. Bring to the boil, reduce the heat and cook, uncovered, for about 10 minutes, until thickened. Set aside to cool.

Knead the dough briefly on a lightly floured surface. Roll out to a 25 cm/10 inch round. Make an 8 cm/3 inch cut from the edge towards the centre and tuck under the cut edges to form a heart shape.

Place the dough on a greased baking sheet. Spread the tomato sauce evenly over the top. Cut the Mozzarella into 10 slices and place around the edge of the pizza, alternately with the artichoke hearts. Cut each anchovy fillet in half lengthways and place two strips in a cross on each piece of cheese. Sprinkle the remaining oregano and parsley over the top. Bake in a preheated oven for 35 minutes until the dough is golden and the cheese has melted.

182 PIZZA WITH MOZZARELLA, TOMATOES AND ANCHOVIES

Preparation time:
15 minutes

Cooking time:
about 30 minutes

Oven temperature:
200 C/400 F/gas 6

Serves 2

Calories:
914 per portion

YOU WILL NEED:
4 tablespoons olive oil
350 g/12 oz tomatoes, chopped
salt and pepper
½ quantity Basic pizza dough (recipe
  159)
175 g/6 oz mozzarella cheese, sliced
8 canned anchovy fillets, drained and
  cut in half lengthways
2 teaspoons chopped basil or oregano

Heat half the oil in a pan, add the tomatoes and cook over moderate heat for 5 minutes. Season and remove from the heat.

Knead the dough until smooth and elastic, then flatten with a rolling pin and roll out to a 25 cm/10 inch circle. Place the circle on an oiled baking sheet. Spread the tomato pulp over the dough, leaving a 1 cm/½ inch margin around the edge. Place the cheese slices on the tomatoes. Arrange the anchovy fillets in a lattice pattern on top. Sprinkle with the basil or oregano, the remaining oil and salt and pepper to taste. Leave to rise in a warm place for 20 minutes.

Bake in a preheated oven for 25 minutes. Serve hot.

▓ COOK'S TIP

This would be a good main course pizza, needing only a green or mixed salad, with any left-over artichoke hearts included, to make a satisfying meal.

▓ COOK'S TIP

This version of the classic Napoletana pizza topping (see recipe 172) uses a different balance of tomatoes and cheese, and adds herbs.

183 SPINACH AND RICOTTA PIZZA SQUARES

Preparation time:
20-25 minutes

Cooking time:
about 30 minutes

Serves 6

Calories:
431 per portion

YOU WILL NEED:
50 g/2 oz cooked spinach
50 g/2 oz ricotta cheese
75 g/3 oz Parmesan cheese, grated
1 quantity Basic pizza dough (recipe 159)
1 egg white, lightly whisked
vegetable oil for deep-frying

Drain the spinach thoroughly and purée in an electric blender or press through a sieve. Mix with the ricotta and Parmesan. Flatten the dough with a rolling pin and roll out to a 5 mm/¼ inch thickness. With a tooth-edged rotary cutter, cut the dough into an even number of 5 cm/2 inch squares.

Put 1 teaspoon of the spinach mixture in the centre of half of the squares. Brush the edges of these squares with the whisked egg white, then cover with the remaining squares of dough, pressing the edges together firmly to seal. Deep-fry the squares, a few at a time, in hot oil until golden brown. Drain on absorbent kitchen paper and serve hot.

■ COOK'S TIP

The Italian word 'pizza' simply means 'pie'; so these little pizza squares are more accurately named than ordinary, open-topped pizzas.

184 KING PRAWNS RISOTTO

Preparation time:
20 minutes, plus soaking

Cooking time:
40 minutes

Serves 2

Calories:
810 per portion

YOU WILL NEED:
450 ml/¾ pint hot chicken stock
½ teaspoon saffron threads
75 g/3 oz butter
1 small onion, chopped
100 g/4 oz green beans, chopped
175 g/6 oz Italian rice
150 ml/¼ pint white wine
50 g/2 oz frozen peas
2 teaspoons snipped chives
1 teaspoon chopped fresh dill
salt and pepper
2-3 teaspoons grated Parmesan cheese
1 garlic clove, crushed
6 king prawns, shelled, with heads on
2 tablespoons brandy

Pour the stock over the saffron and leave for about 30 minutes. Melt 25 g/1 oz butter in a pan, add the onion and fry gently until softened. Add the beans and cook for 1 minute. Add the rice and stir until all the grains are coated with butter. Add one third of the stock and the saffron and bring to the boil. Simmer, uncovered, until the stock is absorbed, then gradually add the remaining stock and wine. Cook for about 20 minutes, until the rice is tender and the liquid absorbed. Add the peas 5 minutes before the end of the cooking time. Stir in the chives, dill, salt, pepper, 25 g/1 oz of the butter and the Parmesan.

Heat the remaining butter in a pan and add the garlic. Cook for 1 minute, add the prawns, season and cook for 5 minutes, until heated through. Pour over the brandy and ignite.

■ COOK'S TIP

Keep the rice warm while cooking the prawns and serve it on a dish with the prawns on top. Feathery sprigs of dill would make an attractive garnish.

185 RICE CROQUETTES

Preparation time:
20 minutes, plus cooling

Cooking time:
45 minutes

Serves 2

Calories:
781 per portion

YOU WILL NEED:
2 tablespoons olive oil
1 small onion, finely chopped
175 g/6 oz Italian rice
600 ml/1 pint hot chicken stock
salt and pepper
50 g/2 oz Italian Mozzarella cheese
50 g/2 oz Parma ham
50 g/2 oz fresh white breadcrumbs
2 teaspoons grated Parmesan cheese
2 teaspoons chopped fresh parsley
oil, for frying

Heat the olive oil in a saucepan, add the onion and fry for 5 minutes until softened. Add the rice and stir until all the grains are coated with oil. Add a quarter of the hot stock and bring to the boil. Simmer, uncovered, until the stock is absorbed, then gradually add the remaining stock. Continue cooking for about 20 minutes, until the rice is tender and the liquid absorbed. Add salt and pepper and leave until the rice is cold.

Divide the rice into six equal parts. Divide each part in half and flatten with the hands to form cakes about 8 cm/3 inches across. Lay a piece of Mozzarella cheese and a piece of Parma ham on one cake and place another on top, pressing the edges to seal. Repeat to make six croquettes. Mix together the breadcrumbs, Parmesan and parsley. Coat each cake in this mixture.

Heat about 2.5 cm/1 inch of oil in a frying pan. Fry the croquettes for about 4 minutes on each side, until golden brown and crispy. Drain on absorbent kitchen paper.

186 RISOTTO RING

Preparation time:
15 minutes

Cooking time:
40 minutes

Serves 2

Calories:
836 per portion

YOU WILL NEED:
25 g/1 oz butter
2 small onions, finely chopped
175 g/6 oz Italian rice
600 ml/1 pint hot chicken stock
salt and pepper
3 tablespoons olive oil, for frying
1 garlic clove, crushed
1 green pepper, cored and chopped
225 g/8 oz chicken livers, chopped
1 teaspoon tomato purée
4 tablespoons dry vermouth
2 tablespoons water
1 teaspoon chopped fresh sage
1 tablespoon grated Parmesan cheese

Melt the butter in a pan, add half the onion and fry for 5 minutes, until softened. Add the rice and stir until the grains are coated in oil. Add a quarter of the stock, salt and pepper and bring to the boil. Simmer, uncovered, until the stock is absorbed; add the remaining stock and continue cooking for about 20 minutes, until the rice is tender and the liquid absorbed.

Heat the olive oil in a pan and fry the garlic and remaining onion for 5 minutes, until softened. Add the pepper and livers and cook until the liver turns colour. Stir in the remaining ingredients except the Parmesan. Simmer uncovered 10 minutes. Stir the Parmesan into the rice and press into a 20 cm/8 inch buttered ring mould. Invert on to a warm plate and fill the centre with sauce.

■ COOK'S TIP

For best results, use Italian Arborio rice. Do not use 'easy cook' rice. The finished, uncooked cakes may be frozen; cook from frozen, allowing 5-6 minutes a side.

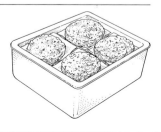

■ COOK'S TIP

The best garnish for this dish is simply parsley. Sprinkle chopped parsley over the rice and arrange sprigs around the outside.

187 BAKED RICE RING

Preparation time:
25-30 minutes

Cooking time:
40-45 minutes

Oven temperature:
200 C/400 F/gas 6

Serves 4

Calories:
768 per portion

YOU WILL NEED:
50 g/2 oz butter
3-4 tablespoons oil
100 g/4 oz rindless streaky bacon,
  chopped
1 large onion, chopped
400 g/14 oz Arborio rice
1.25 litres/2 ¼ pints chicken stock
salt and pepper
100 g/4 oz frozen peas
2 carrots, sliced
2 courgettes, sliced
50 g/2 oz grated Parmesan cheese

Grease an 18 cm/7 inch tin or mould with butter. Heat 25 g/
1 oz butter and 1-2 tablespoons oil in a pan and cook the
bacon until golden brown. Add the onion and cook until soft.
Return the bacon to the pan and add the rice. Stir in the stock a
little at a time, adding more as it is absorbed into the rice.
Season and cook for 15-18 minutes, adding more stock or
water, if necessary, to keep the rice moist. Stir in the peas about
half way through the cooking time.

Meanwhile, heat the remainder of the oil in a pan and
gently cook the carrots and courgettes until tender. When the
rice is cooked, check the seasoning. Mix well and stir in the
remaining butter and cheese. Pile the rice into the prepared tin.
Press well down with a wooden spoon so that the mixture is
firm in the mould. Turn out on to an ovenproof plate and
arrange the carrots and courgettes in alternate circles on the
top. Place in a preheated oven for 10-15 minutes. Serve hot.

188 RISOTTO WITH CABBAGE AND BEANS

Preparation time:
10 minutes

Cooking time:
25 minutes

Serves 6

Calories:
381 per portion

YOU WILL NEED:
200 g/7 oz broad beans, fresh or frozen
1 medium cabbage, shredded
300 g/11 oz rice
salt
75 g/3 oz butter
few sage leaves, chopped
50 g/2 oz Parmesan cheese, grated
freshly ground black pepper

Parboil the broad beans, if fresh, for 2-3 minutes, then drain.
Put the cabbage, rice and a little salt in a large heavy pan with
plenty of water and simmer for 10 minutes. Add the beans and
cook for a further 10 minutes.

Drain the rice and vegetables and spoon into a warmed
serving dish. Melt the butter in a small pan with the sage, then
pour over the rice. Add the Parmesan and a little pepper and
fold gently to mix. Serve immediately.

▩ COOK'S TIP

*Arborio rice is the best rice
to use as it has a slightly
glutinous texture when
cooked, that enables the
grains to stick together. If
you cannot obtain Arborio*
*rice, use a risotto rice or a
long-grained rice, but not an
easy-to-cook one.*

▩ COOK'S TIP

*Use a short-grain risotto rice
for this dish, preferably
Arborio rice. This is a typical
first course (primo piatto)
dish in northern Italian
cooking.*

189 YELLOW RICE WITH PEPPERS

Preparation time:
20-25 minutes

Cooking time:
40-45 minutes

Oven temperature:
200 C/400 F/gas 6

Serves 4

Calories:
852 per portion

YOU WILL NEED:

pinch saffron stamens
3 tablespoons olive oil
1 small carrot, finely chopped
1 medium red onion, finely chopped
1 stick celery, finely chopped
225 g/8 oz Italian sausage, diced
2 sage leaves
2 red and 2 green peppers, cored,
    seeded and cut into strips
1 × 400 g/14 oz can whole tomatoes,
    drained, seeded and chopped
salt and pepper
350 g/12 oz Arborio rice
50-75 g/2-3 oz grated Parmesan cheese

Place the saffron in a small bowl, pour on 2 tablespoons boiling water and leave until required.

Heat the oil and brown the carrot, onion, celery and sausage. Add the sage and peppers and cook for a few minutes, then add the tomatoes and half the juice. Season and cook for about 30 minutes, stirring in more juice if necessary, until the vegetables are tender and most of the juice has evaporated.

Meanwhile, cook the rice in a large pan of boiling salted water for 12-15 minutes until just tender, then drain well, return to the pan and stir in the saffron. Mix in well so that all the rice is yellow; if necessary, stir over a gentle heat until the rice is dry. Stir in the vegetable and sausage mixture and Parmesan cheese to taste. Pile into an ovenproof dish and cook in a preheated oven for 10-15 minutes until golden brown.

190 RISI E BISI (VENETIAN STYLE RICE AND PEAS)

Preparation time:
20-25 minutes

Cooking time:
35-40 minutes

Serves 4-5

Calories:
780-624 per portion

YOU WILL NEED:

75 g/3 oz butter
100 g/4 oz piece rindless streaky bacon,
    diced
1 large onion, chopped
1 tablespoon chopped parsley
400 g/14 oz shelled or frozen peas
pinch sugar
salt and pepper
1.25 litres/2 ¼ pints chicken stock
350 g/12 oz Arborio rice
50-75 g/2-3 oz grated Parmesan cheese

Heat 50 g/2 oz butter in a pan and cook the bacon until lightly coloured. Add the onion and cook until soft but without colour. Stir in the chopped parsley and the peas. Add a pinch of sugar and season lightly with salt and pepper and cook for 2-3 minutes. If fresh peas are used, pour on half the stock and cook gently for 10-15 minutes. If frozen peas are used, add all the stock to the pan and bring to the boil.

Add the rice and mix well together. Season to taste and simmer for 10-15 minutes until the rice is just tender (al dente). If necessary, add a little more stock or some water to keep the risotto moist. When the rice is cooked, check the seasoning and stir in the remaining butter and the Parmesan cheese. Pile into a hot serving dish and serve hot.

▢ COOK'S TIP

You can buy powdered saffron or whole stamens, both used in the same way. If you are unable to obtain saffron, use a little turmeric to colour the rice.

▢ COOK'S TIP

A risotto is usually very moist with a thick syrupy consistency, unlike a pilaff which is a dry mixture. This dish is even more liquid, rather like a very thick soup.

It is served as a first course and not eaten as an accompaniment to a main meal.

191 COUNTRY-STYLE RISOTTO

Preparation time:
25-30 minutes

Cooking time:
35-40 minutes

Serves 4-6

Calories:
616-411 per portion

YOU WILL NEED:
50 g/2 oz butter
2 tablespoons olive oil
1 large onion, finely chopped
2 garlic cloves, crushed
100 g/4 oz shelled or frozen peas
100 g/4 oz small fresh asparagus tips
180-225 g/6-8 oz small courgettes,
    sliced
400 g/14 oz Arborio rice
450 g/1 lb tomatoes, skinned, seeded
    and chopped or 1 × 400 g/14 oz can
    whole tomatoes, drained, seeded and
    chopped
1.25 litres/2 ¼ pints chicken stock
salt and pepper
2-3 tablespoons grated Parmesan cheese
1 tablespoon chopped fresh basil

Heat the butter and oil in a heavy-based pan and cook the onion and garlic until soft and lightly coloured. Add the fresh peas, asparagus and courgettes and cook for 2-3 minutes. Stir in the rice and mix well. Add the tomatoes and the stock a little at a time. Season to taste with salt and pepper. Mix well and cook gently for about 18 minutes, adding more hot stock or water, if necessary, to keep the rice moist. Add the frozen peas, if used, 5 minutes before the end of the cooking time.

When the rice is tender, check the seasoning and stir in the Parmesan cheese to taste. Transfer to a serving dish and sprinkle the chopped basil over just before serving. Serve hot.

■ COOK'S TIP

Any selection of vegetables could be used in this recipe, including French beans, broad beans, sliced mushrooms or peppers.

192 SCAMPI RISOTTO

Preparation time:
10 minutes

Cooking time:
30-35 minutes

Serves 2

Calories:
821 per portion

YOU WILL NEED:
450 g/1 lb green prawns, peeled
850 ml/1 pint 8 fl oz hot fish stock (see
    Cook's Tip)
75 g/3 oz butter
2 tablespoons olive oil
1 garlic clove, crushed
200 g/7 oz raw, short-grain rice (Italian
    Arborio)
good pinch each of ground cinnamon,
    nutmeg and cloves
1 tablespoon finely chopped parsley
3 tablespoons freshly grated Parmesan
    cheese
salt and pepper

Put 65 g/2½ oz of the butter and the oil in a wide, heavy saucepan or deep frying pan and heat. Add the garlic and sauté over a medium heat for 1-2 minutes, then add the rice and stir until golden. Add 250 ml/8 fl oz fish stock, cover the pot, and simmer for 10 minutes or until the liquid is absorbed. Add another 600 ml/1 pint stock and simmer, covered, for a further 10 minutes. Add the raw peeled prawns and continue cooking, covered, for 5-6 minutes longer or until the prawns are pink and the stock absorbed. Gently stir in the spices, remaining butter, chopped parsley and cheese. Taste for seasoning and serve immediately.

■ COOK'S TIP

For the fish stock, put the shells and heads from the prawns into 1.2 litres/2 pints water with 1 fish head, celery stick, small onion, small carrot (all chopped), bay leaf *and seasoning, simmer 30 minutes and strain.*

VEGETABLE DISHES

Fresh, young vegetables feature strongly in the Italian diet. They are served in soups and as *antipasti* and salads. As main course dishes, they are often served stuffed with meat, cheese, rice, herbs and other ingredients. Adapt the recipes in this chapter to suit vegetables which are in season.

193 COUNTRY WOMAN'S SALAD

Preparation time:
25-30 minutes

Serves 4-6

Calories:
302-201 per portion

YOU WILL NEED:
3-4 firm tomatoes, sliced
225 g/8 oz French beans, trimmed, cut in half and cooked
350-450 g/12 oz-1 lb small new potatoes, scraped, cooked and sliced
100 g/4 oz cooked or canned chick peas
100 g/4 oz cooked or canned red beans (see recipe 12)
4-5 spring onions, sliced
1 tablespoon chopped fresh basil
50-75 ml/2-2½ fl oz olive oil
2 tablespoons red or white wine vinegar
salt and pepper

Arrange the sliced tomatoes around the edge of a shallow salad bowl or a deep plate. Pile the potatoes into one quarter of the dish. Pile the chick peas next to them, then the French beans and finally the red beans. (If using canned chick peas and beans, drain them well before adding to the salad.) Sprinkle the spring onions around the edge of the dish and the chopped basil over the vegetables and refrigerate until required.

Whisk the oil and vinegar well together and season well with salt and pepper. Just before serving, whisk the oil and vinegar again and pour over the salad.

194 CAULIFLOWER SALAD

Preparation time:
20 minutes

Cooking time:
5 minutes

Serves 6

Calories:
179 per portion

YOU WILL NEED:
1 cauliflower, divided into florets
salt
50 g/2 oz green olives, halved and stoned
50 g/2 oz black olives, halved and stoned
50 g/2 oz pickled gherkins, sliced
50 g/2 oz pickled peppers, chopped
1 tablespoon capers
6 canned anchovies, drained
6 tablespoons olive oil
1 tablespoon vinegar
freshly ground black pepper

Cook the cauliflower in boiling salted water for 5 minutes; it should still be quite crisp. Drain and leave to cool.

Put the cauliflower in a bowl with the olives, gherkins, peppers, capers and anchovies. Add the oil, vinegar and salt and pepper to taste and fold gently to mix. Chill for at least 30 minutes before serving, to allow the flavours to mingle. Serve the salad cold.

■ COOK'S TIP

If you wish, a crushed clove of garlic can be added to the oil and vinegar. When cooking the French beans leave them slightly crisp so they give 'bite' to the salad.

■ COOK'S TIP

This is a Christmas salad which Italian housewives often add to (or 'reinforce') with new ingredients each day.

195 PIQUANT TOMATO SALAD

Preparation time:
20 minutes

Serves 4

Calories:
235 per portion

YOU WILL NEED:
1 heaped tablespoon French mustard
2 tablespoons white or red wine vinegar
salt and pepper
75 ml/2 ½ fl oz olive oil
4-5 firm tomatoes, sliced
1 stick celery, cut into thin finger-length
strips
1 onion, thinly sliced
1 teaspoon cumin seeds
2 anchovy fillets, chopped
2 hardboiled eggs, sliced

Place the mustard in a small bowl and stir in the vinegar. Season lightly with salt and plenty of pepper and whisk in the olive oil until the mixture is well blended.

Place the tomatoes in a salad bowl with the celery, onion, cumin seeds and anchovy fillets. Pour on the dressing and mix well. Decorate with the hardboiled eggs and serve.

196 CUCUMBER SALAD WITH HONEY

Preparation time:
10 minutes, plus draining

Serves 4

Calories:
194 per portion

YOU WILL NEED:
½ cucumber, peeled and cut into
chunks
salt
2 spring onions, finely chopped
FOR THE DRESSING
2 teaspoons clear honey
2 teaspoons lemon juice
2 tablespoons olive oil
½ teaspoon chopped fresh marjoram
(optional)
freshly ground black pepper
spring onion fan, to garnish

Place the cucumber in a colander over a bowl and sprinkle with salt. Leave to stand for 30 minutes to drain off excess liquid. Pat dry with absorbent kitchen paper.

Combine the cucumber and spring onions. Mix the dressing ingredients together, pour over the cucumber and spring onions and toss together gently.

Garnish with a spring onion fan.

■ COOK'S TIP

Italian red onions are ideal for this salad. They look attractive and have a sweet taste. If not available, use any other type or chopped spring onions.

■ COOK'S TIP

This salad can be mixed up to 8 hours in advance and stored, covered, in the refrigerator.

197 CAPONATA

Preparation time:
10 minutes, plus standing

Cooking time:
about 45 minutes

Serves 4

Calories:
263 per portion

YOU WILL NEED:
450 g/1 lb aubergines, diced
salt
4 tablespoons vegetable oil
6 tablespoons olive oil
450 g/1 lb onions, finely chopped
100 g/4 oz celery, parboiled and chopped
150 g/5 oz green olives, halved and stoned
450 g/1 lb tomatoes, skinned and mashed
freshly ground black pepper
25 g/1 oz sugar
7 tablespoons wine vinegar
2 tablespoons capers

Put the aubergines in a colander, sprinkle lightly with salt, then leave to stand for 1 hour.

Rinse the aubergines under cold running water, then drain and dry thoroughly. Heat the vegetable oil in a frying pan and fry the aubergines until golden brown on all sides. Drain on absorbent kitchen paper.

Heat the olive oil in a heavy pan, add the onions and fry gently for 15 minutes. Add the celery, olives, tomatoes and a pinch each of salt and pepper. Cook for 5 minutes, then add the sugar, vinegar, capers and aubergines. Cook for 10 minutes until the vinegar has evaporated.

198 FRIED ARTICHOKES

Preparation time:
15 minutes

Cooking time:
20 minutes

Serves 4

Calories:
130 per portion

YOU WILL NEED:
4 young globe artichokes
salt and pepper
vegetable oil for shallow-frying

Remove the hard outer leaves, chokes and tips from the artichokes. Flatten the artichokes slightly by holding them upside down by their stems and pressing them against a work surface. Sprinkle the insides with salt and pepper.

Heat enough oil in a large frying pan to cover the base of the pan, then place two of the artichokes in the oil, stems downwards. Fry over moderate heat for 10 minutes, then turn over, increase the heat and fry for a further 10 minutes, turning frequently until golden brown and crunchy on all sides.

Drain the artichokes thoroughly on absorbent kitchen paper and keep hot while cooking the remainder. Serve immediately.

■ COOK'S TIP

This Sicilian vegetable 'stew' is a similar sort of dish to the well known Ratatouille of southern France. It makes a delicious antipasto, served with crusty bread.

■ COOK'S TIP

This recipe is a speciality of restaurants in the Jewish quarter of Rome. Set on a dish, the fried artichokes look like roses.

199 SPINACH WITH EGG

Preparation time:
15 minutes

Cooking time:
10-12 minutes

Serves 4

Calories:
100 per portion

YOU WILL NEED:
1 egg, hard-boiled
450 g/1 lb spinach, washed
25 g/1 oz butter
grated nutmeg
salt and pepper
1 tablespoon lemon juice

Cut the egg in half and remove and reserve the yolk. Chop the white quite finely.

Wash the spinach well and place in a pan with only the water that clings to the leaves. Cover the pan and cook for 7-10 minutes, shaking the pan occasionally, until the spinach is tender. Drain the spinach well and return to the pan with the butter and a sprinkling of nutmeg, salt and pepper. Heat through, then remove from the heat and stir in the egg white and lemon juice.

Transfer the spinach mixture to a warmed serving dish and sieve the egg yolk over the top. Serve hot.

200 BRAISED FENNEL

Preparation time:
10 minutes

Cooking time:
40-45 minutes

Oven temperature:
190 C/375 F/gas 5

Serves 4

Calories:
93 per portion

YOU WILL NEED:
2 small or 1 large bulb(s) fennel,
    quartered
1 tablespoon lemon juice
150 ml/ 1/4 pint hot chicken stock
25 g/1 oz fresh breadcrumbs
1 tablespoon grated Parmesan cheese
1 teaspoon finely grated lemon rind
salt and pepper
25 g/1 oz butter

Trim off any tough stalks and the base from the fennel. Parboil in salted water, with the lemon juice added, for 10 minutes; then drain.

Place the fennel in a buttered close-fitting ovenproof dish and pour over the hot stock. Mix the breadcrumbs, cheese, lemon rind, salt and pepper. Sprinkle over the fennel and dot with butter.

Bake in a preheated oven for 30-35 minutes, until the fennel is tender and the topping golden.

■ COOK'S TIP

If fresh spinach is not available it can be replaced with 225 g/8 oz frozen leaf spinach. Follow the cooking instructions on the packet.

■ COOK'S TIP

The delicious aniseed-like flavour of fennel makes it a good accompaniment for meats like chicken and lamb. It is available all year.

201 PEA PUDDINGS

Preparation time:
10 minutes

Cooking time:
35-40 minutes

Oven temperature:
200 C/400 F/gas 6

Serves 4

Calories:
207 per portion

YOU WILL NEED:
225 g/8 oz frozen peas
25 g/1 oz butter
1 small onion, finely chopped
25 g/1 oz ham, finely chopped
15 g/ ½ oz plain flour
150 ml/ ¼ pint milk
salt and pepper
2 eggs, separated

Cook the peas in a little boiling salted water for 2 minutes, then drain.

Heat the butter in a saucepan, add the onion and fry gently for about 5 minutes, until softened. Add the ham and flour and cook for 1 minute. Gradually stir in the milk and cook until the sauce is thickened and smooth. Add the peas, salt and pepper. Remove from the heat and cool slightly. Beat in the egg yolks.

Whisk the egg whites until stiff. Stir 1 tablespoon of egg white into the mixture, then fold in the rest carefully until evenly mixed.

Divide the mixture between two buttered 450-600 ml/¾-1 pint ovenproof dishes and bake in a reheated oven for about 25 minutes, until the puddings are risen and golden. Serve them immediately.

202 ASPARAGUS WITH EGG AND CREAM

Preparation time:
15 minutes

Cooking time:
20-25 minutes

Serves 4

Calories:
44 per portion

YOU WILL NEED:
225 g/8 oz asparagus spears
2 tablespoons single cream
2 teaspoons lemon juice
salt and pepper
1 egg
1 teaspoon grated Parmesan cheese

Scrape the stalk ends of the asparagus spears with a sharp knife. Tie in a bundle with fine string and place in a pan half-filled with boiling water. Cover with foil and cook the asparagus for 15-20 minutes until tender. Drain, untie and keep warm.

Mix together the single cream, lemon juice, salt and pepper.

Pour 2.5 cm/1 inch of salted water into a small shallow pan and heat to a gentle simmer. Crack the egg into a cup, then slide gently into the pan. Poach the egg for about 3 minutes until the white is just set.

Remove the egg with a draining spoon and place on the asparagus. Spoon the cream over the top and sprinkle with Parmesan cheese. Serve hot.

■ COOK'S TIP

Fresh peas can be used for this dish when they are in season. Weigh them when they are shelled and cook for 10-15 minutes until tender but not too soft.

■ COOK'S TIP

When cooking asparagus, try to keep the tips out of the water, so they are cooked in the steam. This prevents them becoming soggy.

203 CHICORY WITH HAZELNUT DRESSING

Preparation time:
10 minutes

Serves 4

Calories:
60 per portion

YOU WILL NEED:
2 heads chicory
25 g/1 oz hazelnuts, roughly chopped
salt and pepper
1 tablespoon lemon juice
3 tablespoons single cream
1 garlic clove, crushed
2 teaspoons chopped fresh parsley

Separate the chicory leaves and arrange around a shallow dish. Place the hazelnuts in a small bowl with the salt, pepper, lemon juice, cream and garlic. Mix this dressing with a fork then pour it over the chicory.

Sprinkle with chopped fresh parsley.

204 PEAS WITH ONIONS AND HAM

Preparation time:
10-20 minutes

Cooking time:
30-35 minutes

Serves 4-6

Calories:
416-277 per portion

YOU WILL NEED:
8-12 small pickling onions, peeled
50 g/2 oz butter
450 g/1 lb shelled or frozen peas
300 ml/10 fl oz chicken stock
50 g/2 oz ham, cut into strips
salt and pepper
2 slices white bread with crusts
    removed, cut into triangles
4-5 tablespoons oil

Blanch the onions in boiling salted water for 4-5 minutes. Drain well. Melt the butter in a pan, add the onions and cook gently until golden brown. Add the fresh peas and 150 ml/5 fl oz stock and season with salt and pepper. Cook gently for 15-20 minutes until the peas and onions are tender, adding more stock if necessary but allowing most of it to boil away by the time the peas are cooked. (If frozen peas are used, add the stock to the onions and cook until they are nearly tender, then add the peas and cook for 4-5 minutes.) Stir in the ham just before the peas are cooked. Check the seasoning and pour into a serving dish.

Meanwhile, heat the oil in a frying pan and fry the bread triangles until golden brown on both sides. Drain well on absorbent kitchen paper and just before the peas are served, arrange them as a garnish around the dish.

■ COOK'S TIP

Prepare the chicory and dressing up to 3 hours in advance and store in the refrigeration. Dress the salad just before serving.

■ COOK'S TIP

Fried croûtons to use as a garnish or an accompaniment to soups are best if they are fried well in advance and allowed to get cold. They will then stay crisp and are *less likely to absorb the liquid from soup or from any dish they garnish.*

205 BAKED STUFFED MUSHROOMS

Preparation time:
10 minutes

Cooking time:
15-20 minutes

Oven temperature:
190 C/375 F/gas 5

Serves 4

Calories:
190 per portion

YOU WILL NEED:
2 garlic cloves, crushed
1 tablespoon chopped parsley
50 g/2 oz dried breadcrumbs
4 tablespoons olive oil
salt and pepper
12 large field mushrooms, peeled
1 tablespoon chopped marjoram

Put the garlic in a bowl with the parsley, breadcrumbs, 3 tablespoons oil and salt and pepper to taste. Mix well.

Arrange the mushrooms in a single layer in an oiled oven-proof dish, cup side uppermost. Fill the mushrooms with the breadcrumb mixture and sprinkle with the remaining oil and the chopped marjoram. Bake in a preheated oven for 15-20 minutes. Serve immediately.

206 STUFFED AUBERGINES

Preparation time:
15 minutes

Cooking time:
about 45 minutes

Oven temperature:
180 C/350 F/gas 4

Serves 4

Calories:
354 per portion

YOU WILL NEED:
4 small aubergines, cut in half
  lengthways
2 tablespoons olive oil
1 onion, chopped
225 g/8 oz tomatoes, skinned and
  chopped
1 tablespoon chopped parsley
salt and pepper
225 g/8 oz scamorza or mozzarella
  cheese, sliced
4 hard-boiled eggs, sliced
parsley sprigs, to garnish

Prepare the aubergines (see Cook's Tip).

Heat the oil in a heavy pan, add the onions and fry gently for 5 minutes. Add the aubergine flesh, tomatoes, parsley and salt and pepper to taste. Stir well, then cook gently for 15 minutes.

Arrange the aubergine shells in an oiled shallow ovenproof dish and bake in a preheated oven for 10 minutes. Spoon half the tomato mixture into the aubergine shells. Cover with alternate layers of cheese and egg slices. Spoon the remaining tomato mixture over the top, then return to the oven for a further 10 minutes. Serve hot or cold, garnished with fresh parsley sprigs.

■ COOK'S TIP

Stuffing vegetables is a very popular Italian way of turning them into a substantial dish. These mushrooms make a good first course.

■ COOK'S TIP

To prepare the aubergines, scoop the flesh out of each half with a spoon, leaving 1 cm/ ½ inch thick shells. Chop the flesh finely.

207 PEPPERONATA

Preparation time:
20 minutes

Cooking time:
40-45 minutes

Serves 4

Calories:
270 per portion

YOU WILL NEED:
100 ml/3 fl oz olive oil
350 g/12 oz onions, finely sliced
2 garlic cloves, crushed
450 g/1 lb red and yellow peppers,
*   cored, seeded and quartered*
salt and pepper
450 g/1 lb ripe tomatoes, peeled and
*   chopped or 1 × 400 g/14 oz can*
*   chopped tomatoes*

Heat the oil in a heavy-based pan and gently fry the onions and garlic until they are lightly coloured. Add the peppers, cover and cook over a gentle heat for 10-12 minutes.

Add the tomatoes and season well with salt and pepper. Cook, uncovered, until the peppers are tender and the liquid has reduced to a thick sauce. Check the seasoning and pour into a serving dish. Serve hot or cold.

208 STUFFED ARTICHOKES

Preparation time:
20 minutes

Cooking time:
30 minutes

Serves 4

Calories:
264 per portion

YOU WILL NEED:
4 young globe artichokes
125 g/4 ½ oz canned tuna fish in oil,
*   drained and mashed*
4 canned anchovies, drained and
*   mashed*
1 garlic clove, crushed
50 g/2 oz capers, mashed
1 tablespoon chopped parsley
salt and pepper
6 tablespoons olive oil

Remove the hard outer leaves and chokes from the artichokes.

Mix the tuna with the anchovies, garlic, capers, parsley and salt and pepper to taste. Fill the centres of the artichokes with this mixture.

Place the artichokes very close together in a heavy pan and sprinkle with the oil. Add enough water to come halfway up the artichokes. Cover and cook for 30 minutes until tender. Remove the artichokes carefully from the pan with a slotted spoon. Serve immediately.

▓ COOK'S TIP

If canned tomatoes are used, raise the heat towards the end of the cooking time to evaporate the extra liquid. If you wish, the peppers can be skinned before being cooked.

▓ COOK'S TIP

Globe artichokes are very popular in Italy. They are usually very small and tender – an ideal type for this recipe.

209 FRENCH BEANS IN GARLIC SAUCE

Preparation time:
10 minutes

Cooking time:
25-30 minutes

Serves 4

Calories:
132 per portion

YOU WILL NEED:
3 tablespoons olive oil
2 garlic cloves, crushed
1 large ripe tomato, skinned and chopped
600 g/1 ¼ lb French beans, halved
salt and pepper

Heat the oil in a flameproof casserole, add the garlic and fry gently until browned. Stir in the tomato, then add the beans. Add enough water to barely cover the beans, then add salt and pepper to taste and bring to the boil. Lower the heat, cover and simmer for 20-25 minutes until the beans are tender. Remove the lid and increase the heat towards the end of the cooking time to reduce and thicken the liquor. Serve hot or cold.

210 RED CABBAGE BOLZANO-STYLE

Preparation time:
10-15 minutes

Cooking time:
50 minutes

Serves 6

Calories:
185 per portion

YOU WILL NEED:
75 g/3 oz smoked ham, diced
50 g/2 oz butter
3 tablespoons olive oil
½ onion, chopped
7 tablespoons dry white wine
1 large red cabbage, shredded
salt and pepper

Parboil the smoked ham in boiling water for 2-3 minutes, then drain and leave to cool.

Heat the butter and oil in a heavy pan, add the onion and ham and fry gently for 5 minutes. Add the wine and cabbage. Cover and simmer for 40 minutes, stirring occasionally. Add salt and pepper to taste before serving. Serve hot.

▓ COOK'S TIP

Italian cooks always use fresh tomatoes in summer, but will use canned ones in winter. Choose ready-chopped canned tomatoes.

▓ COOK'S TIP

This succulent mixture of red cabbage and smoked ham is excellent served with roast pork. For fine, evenly cut cabbage, shred it in a food processor.

211 CELERY WITH HAM AND BAY LEAVES

Preparation time:
10 minutes

Cooking time:
25-30 minutes

Serves 4

Calories:
90 per portion

YOU WILL NEED:
275 g/10 oz celery
salt
25 g/1 oz butter
1 small onion, peeled and sliced
50 g/2 oz slice of ham, diced
3 bay leaves
freshly ground black pepper
150 ml/¼ pint chicken stock

Cut the celery sticks in halves. Cook in boiling salted water for 10 minutes, then drain.

Meanwhile, heat the butter in a saucepan, add the onion and fry gently for about 5 minutes, until softened. Add the ham and fry for a further minute.

Add the celery, bay leaves, pepper, stock and salt, if necessary. Bring to the boil then reduce the heat, cover and simmer for 12-15 minutes, until the celery is tender. Serve hot.

212 ARTICHOKES WITH PEAS

Preparation time:
15 minutes

Cooking time:
40-45 minutes

Serves 4

Calories:
251 per portion

YOU WILL NEED:
4 young globe artichokes
4 tablespoons olive oil
1 onion, finely chopped
350 g/12 oz fresh shelled peas
75 g/3 oz raw ham or bacon, chopped
salt and pepper
6-8 tablespoons chicken stock

Prepare the artichokes (see Cook's Tip).

Heat the oil in a large heavy pan, add the onion and fry gently for 5 minutes. Add the artichokes, cook for 15 minutes, then add the peas, ham and salt and pepper to taste. Stir in the stock and cook gently for 15-20 minutes, stirring occasionally, until the artichokes and peas are tender. Serve the cooked artichokes immediately.

■ COOK'S TIP

More of a light main course dish than an antipasto, which are generally served cool, this makes a good lunch dish.

■ COOK'S TIP

Young, not too large artichokes are needed for this recipe. Remove the hard outer leaves and the chokes from the artichokes, then slice the artichokes lengthways.

213 TOMATOES STUFFED WITH PASTA

Preparation time:
10 minutes

Cooking time:
about 30 minutes

Oven temperature:
180 C/350 F/gas 4

Serves 6

Calories:
155 per portion

YOU WILL NEED:
6 large firm tomatoes
100 g/4 oz small pasta
salt
2 teaspoons chopped parsley
1 teaspoon chopped mint
3 tablespoons olive oil
freshly ground black pepper
parsley sprigs, to garnish

Cut the tops off the tomatoes and reserve. Scoop out the flesh from the tomatoes, discard the seeds and set aside the flesh. Stand the tomatoes upside down on a plate and leave to drain.

Meanwhile, cook the pasta in boiling salted water until just tender (al dente), drain thoroughly. Put the pasta in a bowl, add the tomato flesh, parsley, mint and half the oil and mix well.

Sprinkle the insides of the tomatoes with salt and pepper, then fill with the pasta. Cover each tomato with its 'lid'. Stand upright in an oiled ovenproof dish and sprinkle with the remaining oil. Bake in a preheated oven for 20 minutes or until the tomatoes are tender. Serve hot or cold, garnished with the parsley sprigs.

214 AUBERGINES PALERMO-STYLE

Preparation time:
10 minutes, plus standing

Cooking time:
about 20 minutes

Serves 4

Calories:
150 per portion

YOU WILL NEED:
4 large aubergines
salt
vegetable oil for deep-frying
freshly ground black pepper

Slice the aubergines lengthways, keeping them attached at the base. Cut each slice into thin strips. Put them in a colander, sprinkle lightly with salt and leave to stand for 1 hour.

Rinse the aubergines under cold running water, then drain and dry thoroughly. Heat the oil in a deep-fryer until very hot, then deep-fry each aubergine separately until golden brown. Drain on absorbent kitchen paper and keep hot while frying the remainder. Sprinkle with salt and pepper and serve immediately.

■ COOK'S TIP

Any of the very small pasta varieties can be used for this recipe, such as annellini, farfallette, or the stelline used in consommé, minestrone and other Italian soups.

■ COOK'S TIP

This simple recipe depends for effect on having fresh, unblemished aubergines. Serve it as a first course with crusty bread.

215 STUFFED COURGETTES

Preparation time:
25-30 minutes

Cooking time:
35-40 minutes

Oven temperature:
200 C/400 F/gas 6

Serves 4

Calories:
458 per portion

YOU WILL NEED:
6 small courgettes, cut in half
* lengthways*
2 tablespoons olive oil
1 large onion, finely chopped
200 g/7 oz Arborio or risotto rice
25 g/1 oz butter
50-75 g/2-3 oz grated Parmesan cheese
2 eggs
2 tablespoons milk
1 tablespoon chopped parsley
salt and pepper

Cook the courgettes in boiling salted water for 3-4 minutes. Drain well. Place under the cold tap until cool. Scoop out the seeds from each courgette half with a teaspoon and discard.

Heat the oil in a pan and cook the onion until it is soft and golden brown. In the meantime, cook the rice in boiling salted water for 12-15 minutes until just tender, or al dente, drain well and place in a bowl. Stir in the butter, half the Parmesan cheese and the onion. In another bowl, whisk together the eggs and milk and stir in the parsley and the remainder of the cheese. Season well with salt and pepper. Stir into the rice mixture and mix well.

Place the courgette halves in a well buttered oven-to-table dish. Pile the rice mixture inside each one and bake in a pre-heated oven for 20-25 minutes until they are golden brown. Serve hot.

216 CAULIFLOWER WITH PARMESAN CHEESE

Preparation time:
10-15 minutes

Cooking time:
25-30 minutes

Oven temperature:
200 C/400 F/gas 6

Serves 4

Calories:
287 per portion

YOU WILL NEED:
75 g/3 oz butter
50 g/2 oz grated Parmesan cheese
3 tablespoons fresh white breadcrumbs
1 tablespoons olive oil (optional)
1 medium cauliflower, broken into
* florets*

Butter the inside of an oven-to-table dish and sprinkle liberally with Parmesan cheese. Heat half the butter in a frying pan, add the breadcrumbs and cook until golden brown, stirring continuously with a spatula. Add a little oil, if necessary, to enable the breadcrumbs to colour evenly. Stir in the remainder of the cheese.

Meanwhile, cook the cauliflower in boiling salted water for 8-10 minutes until just tender. Drain well and place in the prepared dish. Sprinkle the breadcrumbs over the top and bake in a preheated oven for 10-15 minutes until well heated through and the cheese is golden brown. Just before serving, heat the remainder of the butter in a small pan until it is a light hazel brown. Pour over the cauliflower and serve immediately.

■ COOK'S TIP

This dish can be served as an accompaniment to a main course or makes a good starter.

■ COOK'S TIP

This recipe can also be used for fennel or celery. Cut bulbs of fennel into 4-6 pieces and celery into 7.5 cm/3 inch lengths. Cook for 12-15 minutes, until tender.

217 RADICCHIO SALAD

Preparation time:
15 minutes

Cooking time:
6-8 minutes

Serves 4

Calories:
182 per portion

YOU WILL NEED:
2 slices bread
5 tablespoons olive oil
1 garlic clove, crushed
salt and pepper
2 teaspoons wine vinegar
1 small head radicchio
50 g/2 oz mushrooms, sliced
parsley sprigs

Cut the bread into 1 cm/½ inch cubes. Heat 3 tablespoons of the oil in a frying pan. Add the garlic and fry for 1 minute. Add the bread cubes and fry for about 5 minutes, until golden brown. Drain on absorbent kitchen paper and leave to cool.

Place the remaining oil in a screw-top jar with salt, pepper and vinegar. Shake to mix.

Shred the radicchio finely and place in a serving dish. Sprinkle with mushrooms and the bread croûtons. Pour the dressing over the salad just before serving and sprinkle with parsley sprigs.

218 ARTICHOKE OMELET

Preparation time:
15 minutes

Cooking time:
about 10 minutes

Serves 4

Calories:
467 per portion

YOU WILL NEED:
3 globe artichokes
plain flour for coating
4 tablespoons olive oil
salt and pepper
50 g/2 oz butter
6 eggs, beaten

Wash the artichokes, discard the hard outer leaves, then cut off and discard two-thirds of the tops with a sharp knife. Cut the artichokes in half, remove the choke then cut into slivers and coat with flour. Heat the oil in a frying pan and fry the artichokes until well browned. Drain on absorbent kitchen paper and sprinkle with salt and pepper.

Melt the butter in a frying pan, add the artichokes, then pour in the beaten eggs and sprinkle with more salt and pepper. Tilt the pan so that the mixture covers the base. Cook on both sides until set, shaking the pan frequently to prevent the omelet sticking. Serve immediately.

■ COOK'S TIP

The garlic croûtons can be made several days in advance and stored in a covered container. Store the dressing in a screw-top jar.

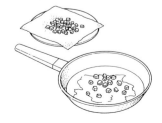

■ COOK'S TIP

The Italian frittata is more of a cross between a pancake and an omelet, rather than a French-style omelet. It is cooked on both sides, and is not folded over. It is usually *filled with other ingredients, especially vegetables and herbs.*

219 OMELET WITH TRUFFLES OR MUSHROOMS

Preparation time:
5 minutes

Cooking time:
10 minutes

Serves 4

Calories:
233 per portion

YOU WILL NEED:
6 eggs
4 tablespoons cream
salt and pepper
100 g/4 oz black truffles or mushrooms,
    chopped
40 g/1 ½ oz butter
juice of ½ lemon
parsley sprigs, to garnish

Put the eggs in a bowl with the cream and salt and pepper to taste. Beat well, then stir in the truffles or mushrooms.

Melt the butter in a frying pan. Pour in the mixture and tilt the pan so that the mixture covers the base. Fry on both sides until set, shaking the pan frequently to prevent the omelet sticking. Remove from the heat and sprinkle with the lemon juice. Serve immediately, garnished with parsley.

220 BAKED MUSHROOMS

Preparation time:
10 minutes

Cooking time:
20 minutes

Oven temperature:
180 C/350 F/gas 4

Serves 4

Calories:
72 per portion

YOU WILL NEED:
350 g/12 oz mushrooms, sliced
salt and pepper
1 tablespoon chopped parsley
1 garlic clove, crushed
2 tablespoons olive oil

Arrange the mushrooms in a single layer in an oiled ovenproof dish. Sprinkle with salt and pepper to taste, the parsley, garlic and oil. Bake in a preheated oven for 20 minutes. Serve the mushrooms as soon as they are cooked.

■ COOK'S TIP

*Black truffles are used in
Italy, but if these are
unavailable or prohibitively
expensive, mushrooms make
an acceptable alternative in
this omelet.*

■ COOK'S TIP

*Leave the stalks on the
mushrooms for this recipe,
trimming the ends if
necessary. Wipe the
mushrooms clean, rather
than wash them.*

SWEET THINGS

Cheese and fresh fruit are usually served instead of a dessert but on feast days and other special occasions Italian families indulge in rich gâteaux such as Cassata alla Siciliana. They eat their renowned ices at any time of the day. In addition to some tempting sweets, this chapter includes recipes for cakes and biscuits.

221 CHERRIES IN RED WINE

Preparation time:
15 minutes

Cooking time:
20-30 minutes

Serves 4

Calories:
357 per portion

YOU WILL NEED:
100 g/4 oz sugar
1 thin strip of orange rind
pinch of ground cinnamon
1 tablespoon redcurrant jelly
150 ml/¼ pint red wine
450 g/1 lb large black cherries, stoned
butter for shallow frying
4 thin small slices crustless bread

Put the sugar, orange rind, cinnamon, redcurrant jelly and wine into a saucepan. Heat gently until the sugar has dissolved, then boil for 1 minute. Add the cherries and simmer gently for 15 minutes.

Melt the butter in a large frying pan and sauté the bread slices until golden on both sides. Drain and arrange in 4 shallow plates. Using a perforated spoon, drain the cherries and arrange on the bread slices.

Reduce the syrup by boiling rapidly for a few minutes, then strain over the cherries. Serve immediately.

222 BAKED STUFFED PEACHES

Preparation time:
20 minutes

Cooking time:
25-30 minutes

Oven temperature:
180 C/350 F/gas 4

Serves 4

Calories:
530 per portion

YOU WILL NEED:
4 ripe peaches, halved and stoned
4 blanched almonds, finely chopped
8 macaroons, crushed
75 g/3 oz caster sugar
25 g/1 oz cocoa powder
150 ml/¼ pint dry white wine
40 g/1½ oz butter

Scoop out a little flesh from the hollows in the peaches and reserve. Mix together the almonds, macaroons, half the sugar, the cocoa powder, 1 tablespoon of the wine and the reserved peach flesh. Fill the peach halves with the mixture and top each one with a small piece of butter.

Arrange the peach halves in a buttered ovenproof dish, pour over the remaining wine and sprinkle with the remaining sugar. Bake in a preheated oven for 25-30 minutes until the peaches are tender. Serve hot.

■ COOK'S TIP

Try serving the cherries on lightly toasted slices of the Italian sweet cake/bread, panetonne.

■ COOK'S TIP

Blanch the almonds by pouring boiling water over them and leaving for 2 minutes. Drain and cover with cold water. Rub the skins off with your fingers.

Do not blanch the almonds until just before you need them as they lose some of their juice when skinned.

223 PISTACHIO ICE CREAM

Preparation time:
20 minutes, plus
freezing

Cooking time:
10-15 minutes

Serves 4

Calories:
517 per portion

YOU WILL NEED:
2 egg yolks
75 g/3 oz caster sugar
300 ml/½ pint milk
75 g/3 oz shelled pistachio nuts, finely
  chopped
175 ml/6 fl oz double or whipping
  cream
green food colouring
chopped pistachio nuts, to decorate

Beat together the egg yolks and sugar until pale. Heat the milk until just below boiling point and stir into the egg mixture. Place the custard in a small pan with the pistachio nuts. Heat very gently, stirring, until thickened. This will take about 10 minutes.

Remove from the heat and cool. Whip the cream until stiff, then fold into the pistachio custard. Add a few drops of green colouring. Pour into a shallow container and freeze for about 1½ hours.

Transfer to a larger bowl and beat the ice cream. Return to the container and freeze for 1½-2½ hours, until firm.

224 PEARS COOKED IN WINE

Preparation time:
10 minutes

Cooking time:
45 minutes

Oven temperature:
160 C/325 F/gas 3

Serves 4

Calories:
242 per portion

YOU WILL NEED:
800 g/1¾ lb firm cooking pears, peeled
450 ml/¾ pint medium red or white
  wine
100 g/4 oz caster sugar
4 whole cloves
pinch of ground cinnamon

Stand the pears in an ovenproof dish, pour over the wine, then sprinkle with the sugar, cloves and cinnamon.

Bake in a preheated oven for 45 minutes or until the pears are tender and the liquor is thick and syrupy. Serve hot or cold.

■ COOK'S TIP

Remember to transfer the ice cream from the freezer to the refrigerator 30 minutes before serving it, so that it softens slightly and is easier to serve neatly.

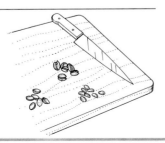

■ COOK'S TIP

In Piedmont the locally produced Barolo wine is most frequently used for this dish, but it is equally good with a medium white wine.

225 SPICED ALMOND CAKE

Preparation time:
30 minutes

Cooking time:
about 1 hour

Oven temperature:
180 C/350 F/gas 4

**Makes one 18 cm/
7 inch round cake**

Total calories:
2,207

YOU WILL NEED:
50 g/2 oz plain flour
50 g/2 oz potato flour
pinch of ground cinnamon
4 eggs, separated
75 g/3 oz caster sugar
50 g/2 oz ground almonds
40 g/1 ½ oz butter, melted
*2 tablespoons amaretti di sarrono or
    other liqueur*
75 g/3 oz plain chocolate
1 tablespoon water

Sift the two flours together with the cinnamon. Put the egg yolks in a bowl with the sugar and whisk until light and frothy. Fold in the flours and the almonds, with the butter and liqueur. Beat the egg whites until stiff, then carefully fold into the mixture.

Spoon into a lined and greased 18 cm/7 inch cake tin and smooth the surface. Bake in a preheated oven for about 1 hour until well risen. Cool on a wire rack.

Melt the chocolate with the water in a bowl over a pan of simmering water. Spread over the cake to cover completely.

226 ORANGE ALMOND COOKIES

Preparation time:
25 minutes, plus
chilling

Cooking time:
15 minutes

Oven temperature:
180 C/350 F/gas 4

Makes about 12

Calories:
155 per portion

YOU WILL NEED:
100 g/4 oz blanched almonds, ground
100 g/4 oz caster sugar
100 g/4 oz candied orange peel, minced
100 g/4 oz plain flour, sifted
6-8 tablespoons milk
50 g/2 oz plain chocolate, melted

Put the ground almonds in a bowl with the sugar, orange peel and all but 1 tablespoon of the flour. Mix well, then stir in enough milk to give a smooth, firm dough.

Roll the mixture into small balls and place, well apart, on a baking tray lined with greased greaseproof paper. Sprinkle with the remaining flour, and bake in a preheated oven for 15 minutes or until golden brown.

Cool on a wire rack. When cold, sandwich the biscuits together in pairs with the melted chocolate. Chill for 1 hour before serving.

■ COOK'S TIP

Make sure that the chocolate has set firmly before you serve this cake. Put it in a cool, airy place, not in the refrigerator where condensation could give a *dull finish to the chocolate if left there for long.*

■ COOK'S TIP

In Italy these deliciously flavoured cookies are sometimes served with small cups of espresso Roman coffee instead of a dessert after a dish of pasta.

227 GENOESE SPONGE

Preparation time:
20 minutes

Cooking time:
about 40 minutes

Oven temperature:
180 C/350 F/gas 4

**Makes one 20 cm/
8 inch round cake**

Total calories:
2,220

YOU WILL NEED:
4 eggs
175 g/6 oz caster sugar
100 g/4 oz plain flour, sifted twice
100 g/4 oz butter, melted

Put the eggs and 125 g/4½ oz of the sugar in a heatproof bowl over a pan of gently simmering water. Whisk until light and fluffy and double its original volume. Remove from the heat and continue whisking until cool.

Add the flour all at once and fold gently into the mixture until evenly blended, then fold in the melted butter. Spoon the mixture into a lined and greased 20 cm/8 inch round cake tin.

Bake in a preheated oven for about 40 minutes or until golden and firm to the touch. Cool on a wire rack. Sprinkle with the remaining sugar before serving.

228 LITTLE CHEESECAKES

Preparation time:
35 minutes, plus
chilling

Cooking time:
30 minutes

Oven temperature:
180 C/350 F/gas 4

Makes about 15

Calories:
242 per portion

YOU WILL NEED:
450 g/1 lb plain flour
4 eggs
2 tablespoons olive oil
pinch of salt
FOR THE FILLING
250 g/9 oz pecorino cheese, grated
25 g/1 oz caster sugar
finely grated rind and juice of ½ lemon
4 egg yolks

Sift the flour on to a work surface and make a well in the centre. Add 3 eggs, the oil and salt and mix the ingredients together to form a soft dough, adding 1-2 tablespoons lukewarm water if necessary. Knead the dough until smooth and pliable. Shape into a ball, cover and chill for 30 minutes.

Meanwhile, prepare the filling. Put all the ingredients in a bowl and mix thoroughly.

Flatten the dough on a work surface and roll out 5 mm/¼ inch thick. Cut into circles, 7.5 cm/3 inches in diameter, using a pastry cutter. Put a little of the filling in the centre of each circle and fold over one half of the dough to enclose the filling. Press the edges firmly together to seal, making semi-circular shapes. Brush each cake with the remaining beaten egg and place on an oiled baking sheet. Bake in a preheated oven for 30 minutes or until puffed and golden.

■ COOK'S TIP

*The Genoese sponge mixture
can also be baked in a Swiss
roll tin until golden and firm
to the touch; then cut into
small squares, iced and
decorated for petits fours.*

■ COOK'S TIP

*Pecorino is a hard sheep's
milk cheese with quite a
distinctive flavour. It is
available in most specialist
cheese shops and Italian
delicatessens.*

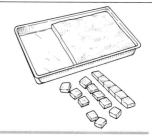

229 STRAWBERRY WATER ICE

Preparation time:
10 minutes, plus
freezing

Cooking time:
5-10 minutes

Serves 4

Calories:
206 per portion

YOU WILL NEED:
450 g/1 lb strawberries
4 tablespoons orange juice
150 g/5 oz caster sugar
4 tablespoons water

Press the strawberries through a sieve, using a wooden spoon. Stir in the orange juice.

Gently heat the sugar and water, stirring, until the sugar has dissolved. Boil for 5 minutes, until syrupy. Cool, then stir into the strawberry pulp. Pour the strawberry mixture into a shallow container and freeze for 3-4 hours, until firm. Transfer the water ice to the refrigerator 30 minutes before serving it.

230 FIG AND NUT PASTIES

Preparation time:
20-25 minutes

Cooking time:
35-40 minutes

Oven temperature:
160 C/325 F/gas 3

Makes 8

Calories:
755 per portion

YOU WILL NEED:
400 g/14 oz plain flour, sifted
150 g/5 oz caster sugar
165 g/5 ½ oz butter, cut in small pieces
3 eggs, plus 1 egg, separated
pinch of salt
FOR THE FILLING
300 g/11 oz dried figs
150 g/5 oz shelled walnuts, ground
150 g/5 oz blanched almonds, toasted and ground
100 g/4 oz seedless raisins
200 g/7 oz marmalade
finely grated rind of 3 oranges
¼ teaspoon ground cloves
1 teaspoon ground cinnamon

Mix the flour and sugar in a bowl, then make a well in the centre. Add the butter, 2 eggs, 1 egg yolk and salt. Work the ingredients with the fingertips to a soft dough, then knead until smooth. Shape the dough into a ball, cover and chill.

Cook the figs in boiling water for 10 minutes. Drain and chop. Mix with the remaining filling ingredients.

Roll the dough to a sheet, about 5 mm/¼ inch thick. Cut into 10 cm/4 inch circles. Put a little filling in the middle of each, then fold the dough over to form half-moon shapes. Moisten the edges with beaten egg white, then press to seal.

Make cuts in the surface of each pasty, place on a greased baking sheet, brush with the remaining egg and bake in a preheated oven for 25-30 minutes until puffed and golden.

■ COOK'S TIP

When strawberries are out of season frozen ones can be substituted, although the flavour will not be as good. Choose a brand containing a minimum of sugar.

■ COOK'S TIP

Soften the raisins for the filling by soaking them in lukewarm water for 15 minutes, then drain.

231 COLD ZABAIONE

Preparation time:
5 minutes

Cooking time:
15-20 minutes

Serves 3

Calories:
352 per portion

YOU WILL NEED:
75 g/3 oz sugar
150 ml/¼ pint water
3 egg yolks
1 tablespoon Marsala, Madeira or
*   sweet sherry*
150 ml/¼ pint double cream, whipped

Place the sugar and water in a saucepan. Stir over low heat to dissolve the sugar. Boil until a thick syrup is formed. Gradually whisk the syrup into the egg yolks with the Marsala, Madeira or sweet sherry. Keep whisking until thick and creamy. Fold in the whipped cream and chill in the refrigerator for 1 hour. Serve in tall glasses.

232 NOCCIOLLETTE

Preparation time:
20-25 minutes

Cooking time:
15 minutes

Oven temperature:
180 C/350 F/gas 4

Makes about 36

Calories:
58 per portion

YOU WILL NEED:
100 g/4 oz butter
40 g/1 ½ oz icing sugar
1 ½ tablespoons honey
100 g/4 oz plain flour
75 g/3 oz hazelnuts, toasted and
*   coarsely ground*
icing sugar for dusting

Cream the butter, sugar and honey together until light and fluffy, then stir in the flour and nuts, mixing to a smooth dough. With lightly floured hands, pinch off pieces of dough the size of walnuts and shape into ovals. Arrange these on greased baking sheets, 2.5 cm/1 inch apart.

Place in a preheated moderate oven and bake for about 15 minutes until firm. Cool slightly and roll in icing sugar.

■ COOK'S TIP

This is a good version of the famous Italian dessert for the busy cook, since it can be prepared a little in advance of the meal. The classic version needs to be served as *soon as it is made as it tends to separate if left to stand for more than a few minutes.*

■ COOK'S TIP

These dainty mouthfuls are an excellent after-dinner biscuit, ideal for serving with strong black coffee.

233 ITALIAN FRUIT SALAD

Preparation time:
25 minutes, plus
marinating

Serves 4

Calories:
202 per portion

YOU WILL NEED:
juice of 4 oranges
grated rind and juice of 1 lemon
2 firm ripe pears or 2 apples
225 g/8 oz apricots
2 peaches
100 g/4 oz grapes
3 tablespoons maraschino
2 tablespoons caster sugar
granulated sugar
pink food colouring
2 small bananas

Put the orange juice and lemon rind and juice into a bowl. Quarter and core the apples or pears; then cut into small cubes. Stone the apricots and peaches and cut into cubes. Halve the grapes and discard the pips.

Add the fruit to the bowl and stir in the liqueur and caster sugar. Place a small plate over the bowl to ensure that the fruit is submerged. Chill for a minimum of 3 hours.

Sprinkle a layer of granulated sugar over a plate. Add a few drops of pink food colouring and stir until evenly coloured. Dip the rims of four large serving glasses in a bowl of water, then dip them quickly into the sugar. Slice the bananas into the fruit salad and spoon carefully into the prepared serving dishes.

234 RAISIN AND CANDIED PEEL BUNS

Preparation time:
about 30 minutes,
plus rising

Cooking time:
20 minutes

Oven temperature:
190 C/375 F/gas 5

Makes 12

Calories:
216 per portion

YOU WILL NEED:
350 g/12 oz plain flour, sifted
25 g/1 oz fresh yeast, dissolved in 2
  tablespoons warm water
2 eggs
3 tablespoons olive oil
salt
50 g/2 oz caster sugar
100 g/4 oz seedless raisins, soaked in
  lukewarm water for 15 minutes,
  drained and dried
50 g/2 oz pine nuts
50 g/2 oz candied lemon peel, chopped

Sift half the flour into a bowl and stir in the yeast mixture, 1 egg, 1 tablespoon oil and a pinch of salt. Mix well, then knead until smooth. Place in a bowl, sprinkle with flour, cover with a damp cloth and leave to rise in a warm place for about 1 hour.

Place the dough on a work surface and knead in the remaining flour and oil, the sugar, a pinch of salt and the remaining egg. Continue kneading until the dough is fairly soft, adding a little lukewarm water if necessary. Add the remaining ingredients to the dough and continue kneading for a further 10 minutes. Divide the dough into 12 and shape into oval buns. Place on an oiled baking tray. Cover with a damp cloth and leave in a warm place until doubled in size. Bake in a preheated oven 20 minutes. Cool on a wire rack.

■ COOK'S TIP

The fruit salad can be marinated in the refrigerator for up to 48 hours if necessary. Do not add the bananas until just before you are ready to serve it.

■ COOK'S TIP

Traditionally fresh yeast is used to make these buns but dried yeast may be substituted, following the manufacturer's directions as to the quantity.

235 CHESTNUT PURÉE WITH CREAM

Preparation time:
35-40 minutes

Cooking time:
1 hour

Serves 4

Calories:
473 per portion

YOU WILL NEED:
450 g/1 lb chestnuts
2 tablespoons milk
175 g/6 oz icing sugar, sifted
pinch of salt
150 ml/¼ pint double cream
2 tablespoons brandy, rum or Strega liqueur

Cut a cross at the pointed end of each chestnut with a knife. Put them in a pan, cover with water, bring to the boil and simmer for 15 minutes. Drain and leave until cool enough to handle. While still quite hot, peel off the shells and inner skins.

Return the chestnuts to the pan, cover with cold water and bring to the boil. Simmer for 45 minutes or until soft. Drain and purée the chestnuts with the milk in a blender or mash using a fork. Stir in the sugar and salt.

Spoon the chestnut purée into individual glass dishes. Whip the cream with the brandy, rum or liqueur until thick but not stiff. Swirl lightly over the top of each portion.

236 RING-SHAPED BISCUITS

Preparation time:
20 minutes

Cooking time:
20 minutes

Oven temperature:
180 C/350 F/gas 4

Makes about 25

Calories:
195 per portion

YOU WILL NEED:
450 g/1 lb fine maize flour
50 g/2 oz plain flour
250 g/9 oz butter, cut into small pieces
225 g/8 oz caster sugar
3 eggs, beaten
finely grated rind of ½ lemon

Mix the two flours together in a bowl and rub in the butter, using the fingertips. Add the sugar, eggs and lemon rind, then knead well together until smooth.

Put the mixture into a piping bag, fitted with a 1 cm/½ inch plain nozzle, and pipe small rings on to a baking tray. Bake in a preheated oven for 20 minutes or until golden. Leave on the baking tray for 5 minutes, then transfer to a wire rack and cool completely.

■ COOK'S TIP

Use canned unsweetened chestnut purée to save time if you need to make a delicious dessert quickly. Try replacing the milk with fresh orange juice.

■ COOK'S TIP

Maize flour is sometimes called cornmeal. It is ground to different degrees of fineness; in a coarser form it is used to make polenta, a speciality of northern Italy.

237 ALMOND CREAM WITH STRAWBERRIES

Preparation time:	YOU WILL NEED:
15 minutes	*100 g/4 oz caster sugar*
	225 g/8 oz cream cheese
Serves 4	*2 tablespoons ground almonds*
Calories:	*2 tablespoons Cointreau*
425 per portion	*450 g/1 lb strawberries, sliced*
	strawberry leaves, washed, to decorate

Beat the sugar with the cream cheese until the mixture is soft and creamy. Gradually beat in the ground almonds, then the Cointreau to make a soft consistency.

Spoon the mixture into the centre of four flat serving plates. Alternatively, press the mixture into a large heart-shaped cutter on a flat platter. Lift off the cutter carefully. Arrange the strawberry slices around and decorate with strawberry leaves, if available.

238 RICOTTA CHEESE FRITTERS

Preparation time:	YOU WILL NEED:
10 minutes	*450 g/1 lb fresh ricotta cheese*
	plain flour for coating
Cooking time:	*2 eggs, beaten*
approx 15 minutes	*vegetable oil for deep-frying*
Serves 4-6	*100 g/4 oz caster sugar*
Calories:	
514-343 per portion	

Cut the cheese into sticks, 4 cm/1½ inches long and 1 cm/½ inch across. Coat lightly with flour, taking care not to break them, then dip into the beaten eggs.

Heat the oil in a deep-fryer and deep-fry the ricotta slices, a few at a time, until golden brown. Drain on absorbent kitchen paper and keep warm while frying the remainder. Sprinkle with the sugar and serve immediately.

■ COOK'S TIP

The almond cream cheese can be prepared up to 24 hours in advance. If the mixture becomes too thick on standing, stir in about 1 tablespoon milk.

■ COOK'S TIP

Ricotta is best eaten as fresh as possible, so buy it from a reputable delicatessen the day you want to use it.

239 APPLE FRITTERS

Preparation time:
20-25 minutes

Cooking time:
about 10 minutes

Serves 6

Calories:
346 per portion

YOU WILL NEED:
50 g/2 oz butter, melted
50 g/2 oz caster sugar
150 ml/ ¼ pint milk
50 g/2 oz plain flour
3 eggs, beaten
1 teaspoon dried yeast, dissolved in 2
  teaspoons warm water
8 dessert apples
vegetable oil for deep-frying

Put the melted butter in a bowl with half the sugar, the milk, flour, eggs and yeast. Beat to a smooth batter.

Peel and core the apples, then slice into thin rounds and sprinkle with the remaining sugar.

Heat the oil in a deep-fryer. Dip the apple slices a few at a time into the batter, then deep-fry in the hot oil until golden brown. Drain on absorbent kitchen paper and keep warm while frying the remainder. Serve immediately.

240 MACAROONS

Preparation time:
20 minutes

Cooking time:
about 20 minutes

Oven temperature:
180 C/350 F/gas 4

Makes about 40

Calories:
83 per portion

YOU WILL NEED:
225 g/8 oz blanched almonds
50-75 g/2-3 oz bitter almonds
350 g/12 oz caster sugar
25 g/1 oz plain flour, sifted
4 egg whites
few drops of vanilla essence
¼ teaspoon grated lemon rind

Grind all the almonds together, using a pestle and mortar.

Put in a bowl with all except 2 tablespoons of the sugar and the flour; stir well to mix. Lightly whisk the egg whites with a fork, then add the vanilla and lemon rind. Add to the almond mixture gradually, until a smooth soft mixture, which holds its shape, is obtained.

Place small spoonfuls of the mixture on greased and floured baking sheets, spacing them well apart. Sprinkle with the remaining sugar and bake in a preheated oven for about 20 minutes or until lightly browned. Cool on a wire rack.

■ COOK'S TIP

Use a pair of scissor-shaped tongs to dip the apple slices in the batter and then to lower them carefully into the hot oil.

■ COOK'S TIP

If bitter almonds are not available substitute the same quantity of blanched almonds and decrease the amount of sugar by 2 tablespoons.